FOOTSTEPS IN THE SEA

Footsteps in the Sea

Adventures with Operation Mobilisation

Deborah Meroff

HODDER AND STOUGHTON
LONDON SYDNEY AUCKLAND AUSTRALIA

To the unsung heroes serving in God's army and navy.

Contents

God moves in a mysterious way
His wonders to perform;
He plants his footsteps in the Sea
And rides upon the Storm.

Deep in unfathomable mines,
Of never failing skill,
He treasures up his bright designs
And works his Sovereign Will.

Ye fearful saints fresh courage take,
The clouds ye so much dread,
Are big with mercy and shall break
In blessings on your head.

Judge not the Lord by feeble sense,
But trust him for his Grace,
Behind a frowning Providence
He hides a smiling face.

His purposes will ripen fast,
Unfolding every hour,
The bud may have a bitter taste,
But wait, to smell the flower!

Blind unbelief is sure to err,
And scan his work in vain,
God is his own Interpreter,
And he will make it plain.

William Cowper

Foreword

'Abandon ship! Abandon ship!'

The cry was like something out of a dream – or nightmare – only this was for real. I could see the captain on the bridge above me braced against the wind, cupping his hands to his mouth. The deck under my feet tilted perilously towards the icy waters of the channel. I felt numb with cold and shock.

How could this be happening? How could the captain order us to abandon our home? *Where – above all – was God in all of this?*

We fought our way to our lifeboats, trembling with distressed awareness that we were abandoning much more than 2,300 tons of steel. Our little ship was the symbol of hope for millions. Surely God would not – could not – let his work shatter on these desolate rocks?

Rescue craft surged alongside our boats, the strong hands of sailors reaching to pull us to safety. And then we saw it. A rainbow, flung in brilliant hues against the dawn sky, arching just above our dying vessel. This, then, was the answer, God's signature to a promise he had given long ago: *Those who put their trust in me will never be disappointed.*

None of us had any idea on that January morning what lay ahead. But this was not to be the end.

1

Casting off

A ship in a harbour is safe,
but that's not what ships are built for.

Author unknown

'There she is!' someone pointed, and with a pounding heart I scanned the horizon for a first glimpse of my new home. Then I saw it – the white hull looming ghostlike in the grey of early morning. The *M.V. Doulos.*

It was 19 January 1986, and twenty-two of us had just reached the end of a long road. For me that journey had begun a few months before with an invitation to join an international Christian agency called Operation Mobilisation. At the break of the New Year I said my farewells to friends and family in Maine, and after stopping at O.M.'s United States base I had flown to join other new recruits at the ship headquarters in Mosbach, Germany.

Now at last the two-week orientation was over, and so was the marathon coach ride to Naples, Italy. Like my fellow travellers I was ready to cast off on our new adventure. Putting first things first we hauled our suitcases, sleeping bags and guitars up the gangway and piled them in the lobby. Then we went in search of breakfast.

The dining room was enormous, capable of seating all three hundred men, women and children who lived aboard this unique vessel. I took a few grateful gulps of coffee, cradling the mug in my hands to warm them. My eyes focused on an unidentifiable object floating on the surface.

'Probably a cockroach,' a veteran grinned, fetching another cup. I swallowed. Back in Germany the new recruits had been entertained with horror stories about these unwelcome stowaways, but I had brushed them aside. Too lightly, it now appeared. What else would I be expected to 'swallow' on this ship?

After breakfast we were paired with 'big brothers' and 'big sisters' who would cushion the shock of our first few days on board. They led us through the maze of corridors or alleyways to our living quarters.

I was agreeably surprised to find only three women assigned to my ten-by-twelve foot, four-berth cabin. Gloria, from Peru, and Liz, from England, were, like me, slightly older than the average twenty-four-year-old recruit. Besides bunks we each had the use of a narrow clothes cupboard and one large drawer of a bureau, the surface of which doubled as a desk. Daylight streamed cheerfully through a porthole high on the outside bulkhead. Like most cabins on this former liner, ours also boasted its own adjoining bathroom.

The *M.V. Doulos* is now certified in the *Guinness Book of World Records* as the oldest ocean-going passenger ship in the world still in active use. Her history is a colourful one. Originally built as a cargo ship in 1914 in Newport News, Virginia, USA, the vessel was later refitted as a tramp steamer. From her base in Monrovia, Liberia, she sailed along the west coast of Africa until World War II broke out. Then the *River Medina*, as she was then named, was enlisted for active duty. The *Medina* was the first ship to meet the German Navy off the west coast of Ireland. In 1941 she shot down a Junker 52 south of the Canary Islands, delivering the survivors to Cape Town.

After the war the battle-scarred veteran returned to the United States to await scrapping. Happily, her old owners came to the rescue and took the warship back to Monrovia for an extensive overhaul. She emerged after months of work with a new name, a new face, and a new career. For the next five years the renovated *Roma* plied the Caribbean and other waters as a passenger liner.

In 1951 the owners ran into financial difficulties and sold the *Roma* to the Costa Line of Italy. The old ship was totally reconstructed and upgraded as the *Franca C.*, providing first class service between Naples and other Mediterranean ports.

By 1977, however, the vessel was definitely showing her age. The Costa Line decided it was time to call it quits. On her last cruise through the Greek islands, the *Franca C.*'s passengers just happened to include representatives of an organisation that was looking for a ship. The *Franca C.* changed hands for the last time.

The *M.V. Doulos*, bearing the Greek word for 'servant', is officially owned by the German charity trust Good Books for All. Since her purchase the *Doulos* has sailed to hundreds of ports all over the world. Those who climb her gangways today find that the former casino and swimming pool have been replaced by conference facilities and a comprehensive exhibition of books for sale. Most remarkably, the *Doulos* is staffed entirely by Christian volunteers who represent about thirty-five nations. All of these young people have committed one or two years of their lives to serving God – and learning how to serve others.

Now I was one of them. I was well aware that a lot of people back home in the States thought I'd gone over the edge. After earning a Master's degree I'd put nearly ten years of library experience under my belt, plus three years editing a mission magazine. I had a good salary and secure future with my own car and house. My second novel was just being published. Why in the world, friends argued, should I throw everything to the winds and run off to sea?

I had no logical answer, really. I only knew there was a voice inside me saying it was time to weigh anchor. If I did not see what lay outside the limits of my own snug harbour now, I would rust in place and it would for ever after be too late.

I was to discover a good many other crew and staff

members who had left established professions to serve aboard the *Doulos*. My friend Mabel, the ship's postmistress, had been a surgeon back home in Argentina. A former successful businessman had exchanged his desk for the engine room, a nurse spent her days in the laundry. Another new recruit, Caroline, was the product of an English boarding school for young ladies. She had spent time at Buckingham Palace as a secretary to the Prince of Wales and now liked to say she had gone from serving the Prince to serving the King.

My own duties would keep me in the communications line: writing up reports of each port's activities to send to supporters, finding stories for magazines, preparing press releases and press conferences, and assisting media people who came to the ship. Later on in Africa there would also be opportunities for holding writing seminars for the crew and public.

To integrate myself with ship life I worked the first month in the book exhibition. It was an unfortunate choice, as both the visitor count and book sales during that period fell to an all-time low. Our ship boasted the largest floating bookshop in the world: over four thousand titles offering a wide spectrum of both Christian and educational books. But reading was obviously not Italy's top form of recreation. The few visitors who wandered up the gangway were more interested in exploring the ship than buying books. Even attendance at on-board programmes was suffering.

Of course, Italy's weather in January and February is not generally conducive to outdoor activities. The exhibition deck was unheated, covered by canvas and only partially shielded customers and staff from icy draughts. Since most of my wardrobe had been chosen with the prospect of a year in Africa, my shivering promptly developed into flu.

For many people Italy conjures visions of romance, flowers and sunshine. For us on the *Doulos* there are other, but just as potent memories: the dramatic spectacle of snow-mantled Mount Vesuvius dominating the skyline . . . our startled introduction to a culture where it is the norm for men to walk arm in arm or hold hands . . . fragrant cups of cappuccino . . . graceful and dignified architecture like Naples's Galleria Umberto . . . narrow back streets with laundry strung out on the balconies . . . irritatingly persistent Romeos . . . and, of course, lunatic drivers.

To our delight, ship leaders arranged a visit to Pompeii for most of us, and for one unforgettable day we explored the labyrinthine streets of that ancient city. Standing in the ruins of the amphitheatre one could almost hear the roar of the crowds, or imagine their screams as Vesuvius rained destruction, overtaking men, women and children in a river of fire.

I was soon to learn, however, that it was the real, live individuals we met during our travels who gave us our greatest joy. Although our denominational and ethnic backgrounds were different, the crew's one common denominator was that we had each established a relationship with the living Christ. We knew what he could do in others' lives because we knew what he'd done to transform our own. And we took pleasure in acting as his ambassadors. The ship provided the perfect platform. *Doulos* conference facilities offered free programmes and films to the public. Teams on shore held programmes in prisons and schools, hospitals, factories and city centres.

Very often we felt a sort of dazed wonderment in what we found ourselves doing. Back home we might never have attempted to speak or sing or mime in front of large audiences. Indeed, we might never have been given the chance. But leaders on the ship believed that after a preliminary grounding in basic techniques the best training was by the 'sink or swim' method. We were thrown repeatedly into situations over our heads and, after some initial floundering, we usually managed to reach inside ourselves and come up with the necessary resources to stay afloat.

A prime example was my first open air programme. Open airs were a favourite method for evangelism with ship members since they could be held almost anywhere and incorporate the talents of any number of people. The usual elements were group singing, a simple pantomime, an introduction to the crew

15

and invitation to the ship, and a short gospel message. The latter was illustrated by words and pictures painted – with more or less expertise – on a large sketchboard.

Most of the crew looked forward to a day of evangelism off the ship every week or ten days. On my first week I accompanied shipmates to one of Naples's great piazzas in what I thought was the role of innocent bystander. Without any warning, however, the Master of Ceremonies suddenly thrust the microphone into my hands with instructions to share something about my faith. I stood frozen; the only thing that saved the day was the eloquence of our Italian translator.

Morale in the book exhibition took a definite upward swing when three ships of the American Sixth Fleet sailed into port. A number of sailors dropped over, and though they didn't buy a lot of books they were as delighted to chat with English-speakers as some of us were. The *Doulos* crew made many friends among the men and even laid on an international music programme for them to explain what our ship was about.

Salerno, my second port of call in Italy and the *Doulos*'s last, was a much smaller and friendlier town. It was easy to be captivated by the dramatic beauty of the snowy peaks rising above red-tiled roofs. Around us, fishermen cast their nets into the green Tyrrhenian Sea, reminding me of home.

In Salerno *Doulos* directors faced a critical decision. The new, more efficient generator we had expected to install in this port was held up by complications at the factory. Should we extend our time in Italy and wait for the machinery, or proceed as scheduled to Malta? The vote was to sail. Instructions were relayed to the factory to forward the generator to Gibraltar – our last stop, we hoped, before heading for Africa.

To our delight local believers took over the *Doulos* galley and cooked the entire crew a farewell spaghetti supper, complete with bread, olives and native mozzarella cheese. The gesture did much to endear Italy to our hearts. So did the fact that on sailing day the sun was, for once, benignly smiling. About ninety friends gathered on the quayside to wave the *Doulos* off after her four-month visit. Some were new believers, introduced to a new life in Jesus Christ through the ship's ministry; others were volunteers who had worked faithfully as translators and assistants in various departments. As the lines were cast off and the water widened between us we could still make out the banner printed carefully in English: 'THANK YOU FOR COMING!'

Like most of the new recruits I was looking forward to my first proper sea voyage. In my blood ran the salt water of my great-grandfather, a Maine sea captain, and most of my life had been spent around boats. I was confident I would have no problem with seasickness.

The *Doulos* waltzed through the Strait of Messina, between Sicily and the mainland, with dolphins frolicking at her bow. By late afternoon, however, the seas had roughened considerably. Those of us who didn't know before learned the difference between pitching (the fore and aft motion of the ship), rolling (port to starboard motion) and corkscrewing (a combination of the two, and by far the most nauseating). I wasn't seasick, I told myself firmly as, one by one, my fellow shipmates turned green; but I did feel better horizontal. Supper that night was not well attended.

Those of the ship's company who weren't working or wishing for an early grave met for the customary evening of prayer and worship. As Associate Director Mike Stachura read the biblical account of the Apostle Paul's shipwreck on Malta, it crossed our minds that we might be in for a re-enactment. All night long doors banged and objects crashed to the floor. The waves were still mountainous the next morning and the harbour entrance was too narrow for us to negotiate safely. The pilot boat stood off, waiting, until at last we had permission to proceed.

Sailing into Grand Harbour, the heart of the island fortress, our misery was replaced by awe. All around us ancient limestone battlements rose starkly against the sapphire of sea and sky. We felt that we had somehow gone back in time. And no wonder. Malta's history layers two hundred and twenty years of Arab domination with centuries of European rule. During the Crusades this small plot of land held out valiantly against the assaults of ferocious Turks. Through both World Wars it served as a key military base for the Allies. No wonder that King George VI of Britain awarded the people of Malta the George Cross, now the country's national symbol; and Queen Elizabeth and US President Franklin Roosevelt both honoured the island as a 'flame in the darkness'.

Today, sun-drenched Malta is a favourite holiday getaway for tourists from all over the world. We had arrived during the island's peak period of rainfall, when it is at its loveliest. During the winter rains the parched landscape blossoms; yellow daisies and ruby red clover spatter lush green fields, and drought is temporarily forgotten.

Malta is by tradition Roman Catholic. At the time of our visit only about a hundred residents called themselves evangelicals. Years before, the tiny evangelical church had conceived the idea of placing a copy of Paul's letter to the Romans – in the Maltese language – in every one of the 80,000 households on the island. Through an unexpected gift the money was provided to cover the printing costs and the books were now in hand. But how could they be distributed? The church needed people – lots of them. And by God's arrangement, the *Doulos* tied up in Grand Harbour at exactly the right moment.

The distribution plan was organised by a man who had met the Lord during a previous ship visit. The idea was to cover the whole country within a single week, Monday to Saturday, in order to head off anticipated opposition by local priests.

Tramping from house to house in the sun and rain definitely raised my respect for the unsung lot of postmen. Some of our copies of Romans were torn up in front of our faces. A few people ran us off their land swearing the book had nothing to do with the Bible. But by the end of the week we felt a great sense of achievement in knowing that 80,000 seeds had been scattered over Malta and the tiny neighbouring island of Gozo. Local believers were thrilled as they began to receive Bible correspondence course applications through the coupons enclosed in each book.

Meanwhile, back on board the *Doulos*, we welcomed 20,000 Maltese into the book exhibition and enjoyed the best book sales of the year. But most heart-warming of all was the response of individuals. The Apostle Paul noted in his account that the islanders were unusually kind, and so were their descendants. Maltese friends twice bought whole milk for the entire crew, and sweets for the children. Local women collected mending that needed to be done and ploughed valiantly through mountains of it.

We had a lot to be grateful for, but when the ship sailed from Grand Harbour we found a 'Thank you' card tacked to the bulletin board from a Maltese teenager named Simon. 'Best wishes for the future,' he had written to the crew, and added, 'I was born again on Friday on *M.V. Doulos*. I feel great!'

So did we. We had enjoyed the rare privilege of following in the footsteps of St Paul – and all without a shipwreck!

The four-day voyage to Gibraltar passed uneventfully. As our ship sailed near the North African coast the crew tossed in bottles filled with Arabic tracts, hoping they would eventually float into Muslim hands. Many of us used our spare time to study basic conversational French. In Gibraltar, O.M. leaders would be making the final decision on whether or not we could proceed to West Africa.

A lot was at stake. The *Doulos* and O.M.'s other ship, the *Logos*, ran largely through the support of international believers; book sales contributed only a quarter of the funds required for daily operation. Over the past year the *Doulos* had barely been able to keep financially afloat. Many predicted that a year in Africa would sink her altogether. Fuel alone would cost $50,000. How could anyone expect a famine-gripped continent to pay the bills? A relief ship loaded with free food and clothing would be welcome. But books? Surely even those Africans who were interested in our books couldn't afford to buy them. And publishers expected to be paid.

Operation Mobilisation would be the last to dispute the

importance of meeting physical needs, but I was glad that it also recognised another aspect to famine relief: the elemental need for hope. Africans were desperate for books. To them, quality educational resources and Christian material represented the keys to a better future.

Months before, O.M. had initiated a project called 'Good Books for Africa', appealing to publishers and individuals for suitable used books in English and French. The response was an avalanche: O.M. received hundreds of thousands of titles in excellent condition and relevant to an African readership. These books could be offered in the exhibition for next to nothing, supplementing the new titles we carried at regular publishers' prices. There would be something for everyone.

By the time we reached Gibraltar, world Christians were beginning to catch the vision. Singapore sent the *Doulos* $10,000 for supplies, two church organisations in Germany each pledged $40,000, and Italian believers raised $3,000. A Dutch evangelical TV station had just assumed payment of $47,000-worth of French Bibles and literature. Other gifts, large and small, flowed in from individuals. The project looked far more hopeful of getting a green light.

Centuries before, the Moors and Phoenicians had used the two-and-a-quarter square miles of 'the Rock' as a staging point for their voyages north. For us, Gibraltar would be the last stop before our long journey south, the end of a two-year, nine-month odyssey in European waters.

Imagine our elation when we learned that tugboat, pilot and berthing fees for the *Doulos* had all been waived. Gibraltar's Deputy Governor, a Christian, assured us: 'We have been praying for your arrival here!' and 150 leading citizens, including the Chief Minister and Chief Justice, endorsed his statement by attending the official reception.

For most of the time we were tied up in Gibraltar I was off the ship in Spain, participating in a two-week training team. The border between British and Spanish-owned land had been open only about a year after sixteen years of non-co-operation. My team was working with an active little church just across the line in La Linea, reaching out to several surrounding towns and cities. Although we came across few English-speakers and my high-school Spanish got a workout, I enjoyed my first plunge into the Latin culture.

The team put in a full day: up at 6 a.m. for devotions, out all morning for open airs and tract distribution, a training session on sketchboards for the church's youth group in the afternoon, and a youth meeting in the evening. When we finally rode the bus back to our accommodation it was usually dark. Once a few rowdy drunks a few seats away decided to be sick all over the bus. Not surprisingly, the ride did little to sharpen our appetites for our host's midnight supper!

Easter in Spain, we discovered, had little to do with sugared eggs and chocolate bunny rabbits. On Good Friday we were dismayed to see a funereal Roman Catholic pro-cession winding through the streets. Black-draped coffin bearers carried a figure meant to resemble Jesus. Because of such heavy traditionalism, many of Spain's evangelical churches tend to avoid Holy Week rituals completely. Some get away from the cities and hold Easter camps. Other congregations stress an everyday celebration of the living Christ and hold services as normal.

At the end of our two-week programme we hiked back to the ship from the border and headed for showers. I was in the middle of mine when I heard my name paged and someone rapped on the door to announce a long-distance phone call. My heart stopped. An emergency at home? My family had tried to telephone only once before, in Italy. Unfortunately they had managed only to reach a Navy ship that was assigned the same number after we left.

I threw on my clothes and, with hair streaming wet, raced up to the information desk. A man was waiting there to show me to the radio tower on the quayside, where the call had come through.

I panted down the gangway after him and he pointed to a 150-foot tower that stretched into the clouds. I groaned. By the time we clambered all the way up the steps I wasn't capable of wheezing out a 'Hello', but the men on duty told me my family had already hung up. They would ring back in a few moments.

They did, quickly assuring me that all was well. The three men in the tower listened with interest to the whole exchange but I forgot their presence. Nor did my dishevelled appearance matter any longer. I was two thousand miles away, on the other side of the Atlantic. For those precious few minutes, I was home!

As a grand finale to our two weeks of training our Spain team hiked to the top of the Rock. It was a splendid day, and a spectacular place to spend it. After a picnic 'on top of the world' and a last longing look at the distant continent of Africa we climbed back down, stopping to take pictures of the famous wild apes, and St Michael's caves.

To the joy of everyone on board, ship leaders were finally ready to announce all systems go for Africa. The crew lined up for the last yellow fever, cholera and typhoid injections and started a course of malaria tablets. On the evening before sailing three truckloads of books and food supplies arrived on the quayside. All available hands formed a chain from the containers to the holds and we managed to stow away fifty tons of goods in little over four hours.

If our arms were black and blue for a few days, it seemed a small price to pay. On 8 April the *Doulos* cast off from the Rock and passed through the 'Pillars of Hercules' to the North Atlantic. We were on our way to Africa!

2

Into Africa

*The darkest thing about Africa
has always been our ignorance of it.*
George H. T. Kimble
'Africa Today: the Living
Darkness', *Reporter*, 15 May 1951

Senegalese Muslims in flowing robes . . . handsome ebony women wearing bright print dresses and headwraps over intricately braided hair . . . the fine art of open-air bargaining . . . lepers begging on the street . . . squalid shacks in the shadow of four-star hotels. Africa was far beyond anything we could have imagined.

Our first introduction to the continent actually came in the Cape Verde Islands, just west of Senegal. The Portuguese who first named these islands were impressed by their green lushness. Today that name is only a cruel mockery. Lack of rain has turned once fertile mountains and valleys into a barren and lunar landscape, carved by ceaseless winds and relentless sun. It is a dry and thirsty land.

Explorer Sir Richard Hawkins wrote in 1593, 'These Ilands are held to bee scituate in one of the most unhealthiest Climates of the world, and therefore it is wisedome to shunne the sight of them, how much more to make abode in them? [sic]'

During the whaling era, ships from New Bedford, Massachusetts, often paused long enough in the islands to

23

pick up crew members. A colony of Cape Verdians was started in New Bedford, Massachusetts, and today there are actually as many living in the United States as in their native country.

Cape Verde introduced most of us on the *Doulos* to a level of destitution we had never before confronted. We had no need for quayside garbage tips in this port. As soon as we carried our plastic bags down the gangway to the barrels, small boys seized them and sifted through their contents. Even empty boxes were considered a treasure.

The thirst of the land seemed to have seeped into the very soul of its people. After the spiritual indifference of Europe, we were stunned when open-air meetings on the street instantly drew crowds of one or two hundred. The first time I helped to give out tracts after the sketchboard message we were mobbed. Adults came running from every direction and children nearly knocked us over in their anxiety not to be left out.

'Will they really read them?' I gasped afterwards to a local pastor.

'Oh yes,' he replied, 'every tract will be read. The people have nothing, so when they are given anything at all, it is highly prized.'

Some may argue that distributing print is an exercise in futility among people who are only 10 or 20 per cent literate. But experience has shown that most individuals who don't read typically find others to read messages aloud to them. Readers are expected to share with their family members, friends, and even whole villages. In spite of the low literacy rate of these islands, the three thousand visitors who came each day to the book exhibition spent an average of ninety-three cents each. Instead of requiring subsidy, we were able to return payment to European publishers for all the Portuguese books we had specially air freighted for this visit.

Knowing that our international music night would draw a large audience we decided to stage the event on shore, erecting a platform behind the high school. We hadn't quite figured on the force of the wind, however: during rehearsal the girls were hard put to keep their skirts from flying around their ears. We doubted that more than a few hundred spectators would brave the elements.

But Cape Verdians were used to wind. By the end of the evening an enthusiastic crowd of over two thousand was jammed into the compound. Most sat on the ground. Several enterprising vendors set up stalls and did a brisk business by lantern light. Simultaneously, hundreds of other islanders explored the *Doulos* book exhibition and attended 'Welcome on Board' programmes. The blowing winds that night could not erode the beginnings of hope.

The ship did not have permission to call in Dakar, Senegal, until the eleventh hour. Our line-up team's repeated attempts to see the Minister of Education, a devout Muslim, had failed every time. In desperation they had at last written to the President of Senegal himself. Almost by return mail, the *Doulos* received a gracious invitation to Dakar.

VIPs who honoured the *Doulos*'s opening reception in Senegal's capital – which has been dubbed 'the boomingest boom town on the continent' – included the ambassadors of Egypt, Poland, Russia, China, Morocco and South Korea. Although the President was unable to attend personally, he sent his representative with a gracious speech of welcome.

This ship was originally built to carry earthly food, now in 1986 it crosses the world transporting spiritual food . . . You are trying to bring a link between people . . . you are contributing to uniting people of different cultures . . . The President of the Republic of Senegal gave me the responsibility of communicating to the promoters and participants of this project his sincere congratulations . . .

All the same, we were apprehensive about moving out into Dakar's streets. The port area was notoriously violent. One of the crew had already had a knife pulled on him and several girls had necklaces ripped from their throats. Ship security was accordingly stepped up. The number of watchmen doubled, and at night gangways were raised and doors bolted.

Adding to our hesitation was our awareness that Senegal was 91 per cent Muslim. The visit of our Christian ship was, unhappily, coinciding with the beginning of the holy month of Ramadan. With religious fervour at its highest pitch we could not expect a lot of sympathy for evangelism.

But as teams launched a city-wide tract blitz our fears evaporated. Muslim pedestrians actually approached us for a leaflet if they were overlooked. If we offered a tract to a fellow passenger on a crowded bus, everyone else demanded one, too – and promptly read it! Car and taxi drivers even stopped traffic to obtain literature. Within three weeks 210,000 French tracts and gospel broadsheets had gone into Senegalese hands. And 1,000 of those who received them had already sent in the enclosed coupons for a free Bible correspondence course.

One day a Korean shipmate and I took a bus to a large teaching hospital where Daniel hoped to arrange a meeting for the medical students and staff. Neither of us spoke French, but Daniel had a contact with one of the English-speaking doctors, and after some trekking from building to building we managed to secure the necessary permission. By that time the heat, dirt, and smell inside the wards – not to mention the bloodstains smeared here and there on floors and walls – had made us rather ill ourselves. One could not help wondering what the survival rate was in such a place.

On our return journey Daniel and I squeezed into a bus already occupied by half the population of Dakar and found ourselves plastered against the back wall. I fought unconsciousness, taking comfort in the assurance that other bodies would continue to hold me upright if I did pass out. Unbelievably, more and more passengers kept adding to the press. When we finally managed to fight our way to the door and hurl ourselves out it was, quite clearly, the wrong stop.

Neither of us had any idea where we were nor could we

ask directions. To make things worse, we hadn't a single remaining franc. So we walked . . . and kept walking. Fortunately, just when we appeared doomed to dusty death God sent his angels in the shape of two nuns. This merciful duo drove us to the general port area and, though we still had a hefty hike to the ship, they earned our undying gratitude.

As a matter of fact, the programme at the hospital several days later turned out to be very satisfactory. Eighty medical students were required to attend so we had a captive audience, though none seemed to begrudge their time. We distributed Gospels of John and other materials at the close of the programme and at least one doctor and her husband accompanied us back to the *Doulos* for further discussion.

Coincidentally, that same day, I sat in on a health and hygiene class that our ship's doctor held for a group of Serare tribe women from the interior. These women, tall, graceful, some with babies on their backs, had been selected to become leaders in their villages. What they learned on the ship that day would be passed on to hundreds of others.

'To you this may seem a small thing,' one explained afterwards in a quiet expression of thanks, 'but to us it is very important.'

I was profoundly moved by the many practical channels God used to show his love. One of my own responsibilities was to handle local media representatives who came to the *Doulos*. Daba was a journalism student at Dakar University, a Muslim. At the end of a long list of questions she had prepared she surprised me with a final one: 'Will you tell me about your personal experience with God?' I was aware of the intensity of Daba's dark eyes as she listened. When she came back to talk again a few days later I was not surprised.

Near the end of our three weeks in Senegal a Chinese journalist arrived with a delegation of forty men and women from mainland China. After the tour he announced that two things impressed him most about our ship: the large number of Muslim visitors – a total of twenty thousand – and the spirit of love he had observed among our unpaid crew.

'What is it,' he asked curiously, 'that allows you to make such a sacrifice?'

I smiled to myself as I answered him, fully aware that we had experienced little of sacrifice. Dakar was only our first port. Nine thousand unknown miles lay ahead as the *Doulos* circumnavigated this great continent. I fervently hoped God would keep his spirit of love shining through each of us.

3
Bush babies

The Gambia is one of the most oddly shaped
countries in the world. It looks like an
earthworm, and fits around the Gambia River
like a long, tight, wrinkled sleeve.

John Gunther, *Inside Africa*

The Gambia was more like the Africa I had always imagined:
hot and steaming, with relentless sun and more than its
fair share of mosquitos. The port of Banjul, located on
a river inlet, had the feel of a small town rather than a
capital city. The buildings were ramshackle, tiny shanties
with corrugated tin roofs. Smelly open drainage ditches ran
along the sides of roads. A fine, reddish-coloured sand blew
everywhere, dusting our white ship and sifting on to our
sandalled feet as we walked.

As it was still the month of Ramadan we experienced
the added delight of dodging the saliva of fasting Muslims,
who refused to swallow any liquids at all. When we gave
out tracts or flyers, however, we set off the same excited
pandemonium in The Gambia as in Cape Verde and Senegal.
Six thousand school children kept the ship's main lounge
overflowing. Every group saw a video tour of the *Doulos*,
and then came an introduction and question time with some
of the crew, a song or two, drama or puppetry, and a
sketchboard story. We were forced to learn fast the best
ways of presenting the story of Jesus to a Muslim audience.

For most of the children the concept of a personal, loving Father God was totally foreign.

As they left the lounge each child received a colourful Good News tract with a form to send in if they wanted to learn more. The book exhibition offered a special packet for about fifteen cents containing a New Testament, a magazine about the ship, a *Doulos* postcard and a tract. The children bought 3,500 of these packets. The fifty donated tons of 'Good Books for Africa' we offered also proved an immediate success.

It was very difficult to leave the ship without at least one or two people, most often children, pleading for a gift; but we met with unexpected generosity as well. The owner of a nearby hotel offered off-duty crew the use of his beach and swimming pool – a much-appreciated oasis.

Now in our fourth African port, we were becoming increasingly aware of the pervasiveness of spirit worship. I was browsing in the market stalls one free afternoon when my attention was caught by an interesting looking necklace. I was just about to start negotiations when the old woman vendor, trying to clinch the sale, exclaimed 'Juju! Good for you!' I dropped the necklace hastily, imagining the sensation I'd create walking into the local church the following Sunday, sporting a fetish.

As our cultural sensitivity increased, so did our respect for the Christian workers we were meeting on this continent. The media love to make sport of missionaries, caricaturing them as self-appointed do-gooders who actually do more harm than good. But the examples of selflessness we saw so challenged us that a number of my shipmates later on returned to Africa to join forces with them.

When we reached The Gambia in mid-May, WEC International offered opportunities for several ship teams to work with personnel at inland mission stations. My photographer friend Susie and I went on the road to follow them up.

Susanna Burton was a vivacious New Zealander who started her career as a staff photographer for a local newspaper and soon graduated to freelancing. When the *Logos* called in New Zealand in 1979, Susie was so impressed by the dedication of the crew that she signed up herself. For three months she served in the galley, washing dishes, then she came into her own as a full-time travel photographer for O.M. By the age of thirty-five she had trekked the Himalayas in Nepal, slept under mosquito nets in the Sudan, and camped on the beaches of Turkey. Susie's love for people showed in her photographs of shepherds and presidents, the wealthy and the destitute, the honoured and the forgotten alike. For the next few years we made a good team.

We spent our first night in the Gambian bush with WEC veterans Hanna Foerster and Emma Wisser, at their mission headquarters in Fajara. Hanna was one of the three nurses who had originally pioneered the work in The Gambia twenty years before, establishing clinics in Fajara and Sibanor, further inland. Hanna was no longer involved in the medical side of the work, but concentrated on training literacy teachers and preparing new reader materials in the local Mandinka language. She and Emma were also finishing the first translation of the New Testament into Mandinka. Susie and I felt awed talking to these women who had chosen to exchange their youth, their comforts and normal desires for the hard life of the bush. Yet they were among the most contented women I had ever met.

We arrived at the Fajara Children's Clinic the next morning in time to watch a *Doulos* girls' team leading devotions with the clinic staff and about one hundred and fifty patients. Afterwards we walked back with the girls to the little house in the village where they were staying for the week.

For most of the team it was a short course in survival: sleeping on wooden cots tented by mosquito nets, learning how to draw their drinking water from a well and boil it. But living in the middle of the community they were also enjoying friendly contacts with their neighbours. It no longer bothered the girls when little children flocked around, excitedly shouting 'Toubarb!' – Wolof for white person. Equipped with a hand-wound tape recorder and gospel cassette in Wolof – the second major trade language in The Gambia – the team instantly attracted large numbers of attentive listeners. And every time the tape finished the audience demanded another replay.

Heidi, an effervescent blonde from the United States, told us about one bystander who had showed no interest in listening.

> He spoke in English and asked us why we had come to bring a white man's religion. I explained that we had come to share about a person, not a religion; that Jesus himself was not 'white', and his news was for all men.
>
> The man told us he found no satisfaction in Islam or any religion that he knew of. He asked many questions and we were amazed to find the Lord really putting words in our mouth. Verses I had memorised came to me without thinking. He listened seriously to everything we said and when we offered to sell him a Bible at a nominal cost he accepted eagerly. We're believing that God will answer this man's questions as he reads.

Li Wah from Singapore had been able to share with an elderly Muslim woman how she had given up idol worship when she accepted Jesus. To her surprise the old woman promptly removed the charms from around her neck, declaring she didn't want them any more either.

What impressed this *Doulos* team most were the lives of the mission workers. 'It was an awakening about what true missionaries go through,' Heidi confided. 'God really worked miracles for Hanna and the others to start this clinic. We know none of the missionaries can be here on their own strength.'

Margaret regarded her contact with Emma and Hanna as a small miracle. Back home in Papua New Guinea she had once selected a mission prayer card at random and begun praying for two women engaged in translation work in Africa. To her astonishment, on the Fajara team, she was introduced to these very missionaries.

Shirley Strong, WEC Field Leader for The Gambia, met Susie and I around 8.30 a.m. and we continued in her car to Sibanor, the main medical station. The drive took us through flat, dry savannah dotted with palms and scrub trees. Miles of shanties covered with corrugated metal roofs gave way to round thatched huts. Now and then a large mosque loomed prominently. Sheep, goats, or cows wandered across the road and Shirley blew her horn to clear the way. Once she pulled over to let us examine a curiously elongated termite hill that towered above our heads.

By the time we reached Sibanor the heat was staggering. We were introduced to Dr Gisela Schneider, a slim, dark-haired young woman who radiated a quiet happiness. Only twenty-eight years old, Dr Gisela was in charge of all the WEC medical work in the country. Two hundred thousand patients had been seen by the four centres in the last year. Sibanor alone treated a daily total of four to five hundred patients – and up to seven hundred during the rainy season.

Our three women from the *Doulos* were bursting with tales of bush clinic life. Elisabeth, who had trained as a nurse in a state-of-the-art hospital in Switzerland, was still in a state of shock. She described a typical day: 'Ten patients at a time crowd into the little examining room. The nurses select those who must see the doctor and treat the rest themselves. It all went so fast I don't know how they could do it; but it was the only way they *could* do it.'

Ulrike, another nurse, had known Gisela Schneider back home in Germany, and had prayed for the Sibanor clinic: 'But seeing it in reality is completely different.'

Before beginning each work day, Dr Gisela made it a practice to meet with all the waiting patients and share Scripture verses with them in native Mandinka. Through such clinics many thousands had heard the good news about Jesus Christ. Although few converts had emerged in this Muslim stronghold, seeds were sown that the staff believed would one day ripen to faith.

The Sibanor clinic had already established a reputation for

its loving concern for the Mandinka, Fula, Jula and other tribes. Often, when a villager was seriously injured, his friends would carry him many miles, by-passing other clinics, to get him to Sibanor. Other local people, sadly, refused to go to any clinic for help because they were forbidden by the powerful head man or *Maribu*. Their lives were circumscribed by dread. Amulets or fetishes were worn universally for protection against the spirits, even hung around the necks, arms or waists of the tiniest babies. Huts were built in the round so that spirits had no corners in which to hide.

Elisabeth was particularly distressed at the lot of women. She explained how little girls underwent crude circumcision rites when they were only seven or eight years old, then married as soon as they reach child-bearing age. 'Women are only considered useful as long as they produce children. There were 757 deliveries at Sibanor last year. Women walk long distances, often in labour, to have their babies at the clinic. A few hours later they are on their way home again. But the infant mortality rate is very high.'

Ulrike told about their first evening, when a mother brought a baby suffering from meningitis. 'The baby died. Only last week its brother died from the same disease. The next day we saw a baby that had been terribly burned. The mother did not bring her in for treatment until a week after the accident!'

The *Doulos* team's third member, Mabel, was a qualified doctor from Argentina. She told us the clinic saw over ninety-five expectant women in one day. 'Some women say they want something done to them so they will have no more children. They want a rest. Others come to plead for a way to have another child, because their husbands are threatening to take another wife if they don't.'

Diseases rarely seen in the West such as tuberculosis and malaria were common killers in The Gambia. With the breakdown of traditional morality, sexually transmitted diseases were also rampant. The local *Maribu* had even gone so far as to declare that any boy who reached fifteen or sixteen without contracting such a disease wasn't

34

a man! During our tour of the clinic, Susie and I were shown an infant who had been born with syphilis. He lay shrunken and still, close to death.

'What touched me most,' Mabel confessed, 'was seeing how Gisela looked at her patients with love, no matter how busy she was. She knows she's doing God's will and she's happy. This experience has been a push for me. It's shown me that I have to get my priorities straight.'

We travelled on to the Sibanor Youth Centre and Jarrol clinic further upriver before returning to Banjul. I noticed that in the comparative cool of the mission house the thermometer registered 96 degrees Fahrenheit; it must have been 110 or 120 degrees in the sun. As the resident missionary proudly showed us her little garden and chickens she murmured, 'We used to have more chickens, but the snakes got them.' I decided I wasn't cut out for The Gambia.

Life in this neglected pocket of Africa was more than any of us had bargained for. Before she left, the *Doulos* made sure that spare medical supplies got to the clinics, and books from the exhibition would supplement the scattered lending libraries at the youth centres and stations. But it was easy to see how much more needed to be done in this forgotten land, and how pitifully few there were committed to do it. 'Without a vision, the people perish,' God tells us in his Word. It is as simple – and as tragic – as that.

4

Where ignorance is not bliss

If it were not for hope,
the heart would break.

English proverb, c. 1200

In order to reach Guinea Bissau's capital city we had to leave
the Atlantic coast and nose our way for five hours up a wide,
sandy canal. Bissau had just one deepwater berth and the
Minister of Transport could not guarantee it to a bookship.
The country was desperately dependent on transfusions of
outside aid. If another vessel arrived with food we would
have to move out. We decided it was worth the risk.

Local believers had met together every week for a year
to pray for this visit. On arrival day two hundred gathered
on the quayside and waited patiently for two hours under a
scorching sun. As the ship came into sight they burst into
jubilant cheers, singing and clapping and dancing for joy,
holding their welcome banners high.

After hearing so much about the extreme poverty of Guinea
Bissau, our first walk into town was a surprise. The streets
were wide and paved, the buildings modest but respectable
looking. There were even one or two modern hotels. Then we
took a closer look. Most of the shops wore a silent air of aban-
donment. The entrances to some of the hotels and restaurants
were locked and shuttered. Stepping into a furniture store I
saw only a few chairs and a bed standing forlornly in the
centre of a large expanse of floor. Bissau was a ghost town.

For the last six weeks there had been no fuel. Transportation had come to a halt, even fishing boats couldn't leave port. An already hungry nation got hungrier. The city's open markets swarmed with people, but there was little for sale besides mangoes and a few sweet potatoes. Along the road we saw people picking cashew fruit from the trees. The fruit has a high protein value but it was used to produce the local wine more often than it was eaten. Cashew wine was the poor man's escape from a hopeless existence.

Riding out to a pineapple plantation with the chief steward one day we discovered that outside the city proper the paved streets degenerated into badly potholed dirt roads. Concrete buildings were replaced by houses of mud bricks and thatch. Women, obviously the burden-bearers in this society, walked by the side of the dusty road with an infant strapped to their backs and a large bucket or basket balanced atop their heads. As often as not they also carried the weight of an unborn child.

It was said that girls born into the Papel tribe further into the interior could expect to be married by the age of eleven. Physically unprepared for childbirth, these girls usually miscarried their first pregnancies. Of the ten or twelve children they might eventually produce, an average of two or three might survive the everyday hazards of malaria, meningitis, leprosy, TB – and hunger.

The pineapples at the plantation turned out to be too green for our steward, Miles, to buy, but mangoes were ripe and ready. We loaded up 500 kilos and topped them off with a supply of coconuts and lemons.

That Sunday of our only weekend in Guinea Bissau I squeezed on to the wooden benches of a native church with 150 other believers. The corrugated metal roof overhead contained the heat like an oven, and although the unscreened windows were wide open I could feel sweat trickling steadily down my back. Dozens more children and adults peered in from outside, their elbows propped on the window sills. But the lively Portuguese creole music, accompanied by clapping and tambourines in a strong African rhythm, more than made up for the discomfort. Together we celebrated a communion supper of bread and cashew nut wine that was, to the embarrassment of the local missionary, more than a little potent.

In the afternoon I returned to the same village with an open-air team. We set up our sketchboard in the middle of thatched huts, underneath a mango tree. Besides interested pigs, goats and chickens we gathered a 'standing room only' crowd of a hundred men, women and children. Many of the little ones who pressed close to the front were naked, their legs and arms stick-like and stomachs distended by malnutrition.

What right did we have, we asked ourselves, to offer only words in the face of such obvious physical need? The answer emerged as we saw for ourselves the many families who raised livestock, not to eat, but to offer as sacrifices to the spirits. Their way of life from birth to death was dictated by fear. Even their huts were made without openings for light, to prevent spirits entering in. In dramatic contrast, those who had accepted Christ's sacrifice in place of the offering of pigs and goats were living in comparative health and happiness.

As with every other place we visited in West Africa, we discovered that even a crippling poverty had not succeeded in crushing the desire to learn. By the end of five days the people of Guinea Bissau had purchased nine thousand New Testaments, offered at a cost representing an hour's wage. A representative of the Ministry of Culture wanted to buy all of the Portuguese titles we carried in order to start a library in Bissau. Although we had to reserve some of the stock for the public he was able to purchase hundreds of quality titles. We also supplied a few vanloads to the country's only Christian bookshop, run by WEC missionaries. Daily sales in the book exhibition actually totalled six times what they had been in Italy! The only problem was converting local pesos to hard currency so that we could pay the book bills back in Europe.

The *Doulos* untied from her berth in Bissau at seven o'clock on a June morning. Even at high tide we had a draught of only a few metres, and our propellor churned up the silt of the river bed. A cargo ship would take our place almost as soon as we moved away. Queues of hungry people were already forming to wait for whatever was on offer.

But as I stood at the rail waving to the large number of volunteers, local believers and missionaries who had gathered at this early hour to see us off, I was deeply moved. For these people had come not only to say farewell to us, but to give thanks to God – thanks for sending a cargo of infinite value to this stricken nation: a cargo of hope.

5

Acquired tastes

In Africa think big.
Cecil Rhodes, attributed

Plain mangoes, mango jam, mango pudding, mango cake, mango crumble and, just for a dash of variety, mango ice cream. At first we greeted our steward's generous purchase of this exotic fruit with enthusiasm; we looked forward with some humour to whatever our creative galley staff would come up with next. But then the novelty wore off. A few of us were fast developing mangled stomachs. Several others swelled up or broke out in rashes. But mangoes, we decided philosophically, were all part of the Africa experience. Like goat meat – and fu-fu.

Fu-fu is a dough-like substance made from yams, in taste and texture resembling wallpaper paste. Dear to the heart of West Africans, fu-fu is usually served up with palm nut oil in a fiery hot sauce, and rice. I ate it almost every Sunday that I was on a church team ashore, and I was invariably sick.

Well do I remember my initiation into fu-fu at a pastor's table. The oppressive heat and flies swarming around us in clouds did not contribute to a robust appetite. I had just stoically managed, however, to choke down a whole sticky white plateful when the pastor's wife smilingly deposited another mountain of the stuff in front of me. I swallowed hard. To refuse hospitality would cause offence, but I was dead certain that being sick all over the table wouldn't do much for the cause of friendship either. I forced myself to eat, mouthful by mouthful – and paid for it as soon as we got back to the ship.

In spite of the precautions we took like soaking fresh fruits and vegetables in solution, intestinal upsets of all sorts were a part of everyday life in West Africa. By the third or fourth port, cramps and 'runny tummy' were so commonplace that most of us gave up reporting to the clinic and just slogged on, fasting and drinking quantities of fluid with sugar and salt to avoid dehydration. We knew we'd be fortunate if this was our only complaint. The local papers in Sierra Leone were reporting three to four thousand cases of cholera, with 350 deaths. A crew member preparing the way for the *Doulos* in Ghana had chicken pox, and another line-up man on the Ivory Coast was down with malaria.

I was learning a lot about Africa. Like many who have never been to this marvellous continent I had naively pictured the whole of it as all pretty much the same. As we sailed from port to port around the enormous land mass, however, we were presented with striking variations, not only in the face of the land but in the appearance of the people: height and body structure, facial markings, shades of skin. The languages of each country also offered mind-boggling variety. Besides the official tongues of English, French or Portuguese, a single nation could use seventy or eighty or even a hundred tribal dialects. It was not uncommon in some of our programmes to have translations into two languages – always a challenge to the speaker, who had to remember what he was saying when it came around to his turn again.

Obviously the ship couldn't offer books in all of the languages we encountered. As much as possible we added stocks of local literature to our own. But in all too many cases there was nothing at all available in print, not even portions of the Bible. This sad discovery added fuel to my determination to encourage nationals to write. Translated books were fine, and so were the occasional visits of a bookship; but in the long term these developing nations required national writers.

They alone could most effectively address specific cultural issues, using the natural idioms of their people groups.

I held eight Writers' Workshops in Africa. The first was in Sierra Leone. Although the programme had been well publicised on national radio, we had no idea what sort of response we'd get. The first evening half a dozen women wandered into the conference room with crying toddlers, one mother complacently breastfeeding her infant. After a volunteer announced the subject of the workshop a number hastily got up and disappeared. Seventy-nine of my audience stuck it out, however; a healthy cross-section of men and women of all ages and interests, and all keen to learn.

That first night our group talked over personal goals, motivation and discipline, basic tools and resources, finding ideas and getting them organised. I asked in which areas they felt their country most urgently lacked material in local languages. Children's stories? Self-help or advice articles about marriage or the family? Sunday School lessons? Tracts? *All of these*, they assured me. Sierra Leone had a dearth of material on every subject, on every level. As we talked their excitement caught fire. They began to understand that the field of opportunities was wide open. Even if they weren't yet accomplished writers, even if they had limited access to printing or publishing resources, they could make a start.

The same group met the second night to concentrate on general writing techniques. During the third session we touched briefly on different types of writing – fiction and non-fiction, articles and stories, news writing. Class members were invited to arrange tutorials with me on an individual basis throughout the week.

Although such workshops were too brief to accomplish a great deal, I believe that at the very least African men and women were encouraged to attack the challenge in front of them. I hope and pray that some are now beginning to fill the gaps.

The President of Sierra Leone and his entourage had been the first to pay the *Doulos* an official visit; a total of 92,000 surged up the gangways in their wake. On each of our weekends in Freetown a long line of people twisted far down the quay and out of sight to the port gate.

Roberto from Italy was one of the men assigned to keep the crowds in control. It wasn't an enviable job, especially under the blaze of the afternoon sun. Roberto confessed that when one day someone snatched his valuable watch, the accumulated fatigue and frustration boiled over. He took a few minutes off to try to pull himself together. Thinking about the compassion Jesus showed crowds somehow gave Roberto the determination to go back.

None of us on board were superheroes. Emotionally we often felt raw and vulnerable, sickened by injustices or poverty that we could do nothing about. Apart from the central business district of the city, Freetown made little pretence of prosperity. Open drains ran down both sides of the streets. Unpaved shantytowns made of scraps of tin scarred the hillsides. The few pavements were usurped by vendors selling fly-covered fruits and vegetables and everything else, literally, under the sun.

When my cabinmate Gloria and I once took a wrong turn into a Muslim neighbourhood we could feel the eyes of householders boring into us with almost tangible hostility. We quickened our pace, but not before a clod of dirt sailed past our heads. Another *Doulos* woman was sitting in a van stalled in traffic when a man came to the window and spat into her face.

In spite of such incidents we saw an unprecedented response to open-air preaching. None of us who witnessed it are likely to forget the sight of the hundreds who knelt to pray in the streets of the city centre. Was it only mass hysteria? A Scripture Union representative later wrote to tell us that a large number of those who had publicly committed themselves to Jesus Christ in open-air meetings were attending new Bible study groups in various parts of Freetown. For some, at least, the decision had been real.

At sunrise on the morning before we sailed I stood on a

nearby beach for a special ceremony. Two brothers, Ibrahim and Idrissa, had originally come to the ship to argue against Christianity. After several long discussions the young men took away a New Testament with the sole intent of finding 'holes' in the Scriptures. As they began reading about the life of Christ, however, something quite unexpected happened. Ibrahim and Idrissa fell in love with the main character. They were aware of the possible danger, but decided they had to make public their conversion from following Mohammed to following Jesus Christ. With their new brothers and sisters from the *Doulos* standing as witnesses, Ibrahim and Idrissa 'died' to their old lives in the waters of baptism, and arose to the greatest challenge they would ever face.

The continent of Africa has never been entirely free of political and economic upheaval. Many governments are in transition, and Liberia, the next stop on our schedule, was at that time dangerously close to civil war. Samuel Doe's presidency had been secured by a bloody military coup some years before. Now that he himself had just emerged from a coup against his government, Doe wasn't taking any chances. The capital city of Monrovia was an armed camp, with soldiers everywhere. The *Doulos* went ahead with its visit only after considerable debate.

Almost as soon as we docked, security officers descended for a bow to stern search. Sierra Leone had been accused of backing the recent coup, so we were advised not to advertise the fact that Freetown was our last port of call. Naturally, that was the first question I was asked at our opening press conference. I was still sweating out a tactful reply when another reporter belligerently suggested that our book exhibition was nothing more than a fence for our real anti-government activities!

With this kind of rampant suspicion, no one was terribly surprised when the *Doulos* was closed down a few days later for a second search. No coming or going was allowed for almost a day while two dozen officials from the national security council conducted a cabin-to-cabin inspection. Naturally they came up with nothing, and the publicity only served to increase the number of visitors.

We soon got very nonchalant about halting at checkpoints and roadblocks wherever we went in Monrovia. When police and soldiers finished off the usual interrogation with a suggestive, 'What do you have for us, boss?' we always produced tracts and offered low cost Bibles or other literature. Sales boomed!

One day the chairman of the local *Doulos* committee took Susie, Captain and Mrs Isaacson and me out to visit one of our teams at a leprosy centre several hours away. For me the long and enjoyable drive through lushly fertile countryside was marred by apprehension. The Ganta Leprosy Centre was one of very few facilities addressing a widespread problem in Africa. In almost every port we had been troubled by the sight of lepers, the mentally disturbed, and other individuals who were seriously afflicted but untreated, roaming the streets. There just didn't seem to be enough doctors, hospitals and medicines to go around.

Most readers will be aware that leprosy is, like AIDS, an immune deficiency disease. Unless the 'right' germs come along to trigger the disease, people might never know they carry it. In the Western world early identification and treatment usually ensures there is no obvious sign of leprosy. In Africa, however, early detection is seldom possible and options for treatment are limited. Some victims have even, sadly, deliberately allowed themselves to be disfigured in order to attract more alms. At the Ganta centre we would doubtless be exposed to the worst ravages of the disease – the missing limbs, fingers and toes, the grotesque features. How would I handle it? How were my shipmates handling it?

As we soon learned, even though Ganta had only one doctor to superintend treatment for 400 residents, it was a place of hope. Many patients were allowed to live in tiny houses with their whole families. All who were able to work were expected to raise food, tend animals or create woodcarvings to sell. Members of the Peace Corps, the

US government agency that helps developing nations with agricultural and educational projects, were showing residents how to develop a self-supporting farm. Participation in their own well-being made all the difference.

Our twenty-four crew members from the *Doulos* were lending their muscle for two weeks of ditch-digging, field-clearing, and planting of banana and papaya trees. Some of the team constructed rabbit hutches over water so the animals wouldn't be eaten by driver ants. One or two qualified nurses helped in the hospital. Their sense of fulfilment was evident, but the best part, everyone agreed, was spending time with individual patients. They had learned that disfigurement was no barrier to friendship.

Several days after our return from the leprosy centre, Susie and I accompanied an expedition to a rubber plantation outside Monrovia. This Firestone plantation was reputed to be the largest in the world, encompassing nine million trees and 100,000 resident workers and their families. A *Doulos* deck crew was helping to renovate a house for a family from SIM (the Society for International Ministries) that had received permission to work among them.

While most of the men got to work with the 'house raising', the rest of us went with the missionary to visit several of the plantation's ninety-four communities. On the way he stopped in the forest to give us a closer look at the rubber trees.

Each plantation employee, our guide explained, was responsible for 600 trees, tapping 200 per day. He pointed out the small metal cups that hung under taps inserted into the slender trunks. Peering into one of them we could see a milky liquid resembling glue. A chemical would be added to this latex to prevent it from hardening. The rubber would then be shipped in both liquid and solid forms to Firestone's processing plants in the States.

At least a hundred Liberian workers and their families gathered for the open-air programme that afternoon; we had a great time together singing songs with the children and telling them a little about our ship. That night, in another camp miles away, we met by lantern light.

The magical scene is still carved on my memory: the cool, clear evening, untroubled by mosquitos; dots of light from the village houses and open fires surrounding us; and, coming from far away, the throb of a drum. The missionary stood with a lamp on one side of our First Mate, lighting Andrew's Bible as he spoke. On his other side, a Liberian believer translated Andrew's words into Pele. I wondered if the earliest missionaries to Africa might not have enacted similar scenes, a century, even two centuries before.

Walking through deep forest on our way back to the truck, the missionary held our attention with stories of the spirit worship that was still strong in the area. Tribal religions with secret societies held a grip on many of the plantation workers, he said, and primitive rites – even human sacrifice – were known to take place. We glanced uneasily at the tall trees towering above us like ghostly sentinels. The forest was so pitch black we couldn't see the path. I wished devoutly that the missionary had chosen another moment for his stories. So did the others, judging by the speed with which they vaulted into the truck when we finally reached it.

The contemporary mind likes to put such anomalies as human sacrifice tidily away into an ancient history file. Knowing that they still exist is disconcerting. We had a similar experience leaving Liberia in mid-July, on the way to the Ivory Coast. It was prime sailing weather and the *Doulos* had already put a good number of sea miles behind her when we suddenly became aware of perhaps a dozen small fishing boats, spaced in a distant circle around us. One of the boats came close enough for an officer on the bridge to pick it out clearly with binoculars. A half-covered pile of grappling hooks was lying on its deck. And waving, unbelievably, from its mast was a pennant bearing skull and crossbones. The boats belonged to modern-day pirates, lying in wait for ships they knew were scheduled to pass.

Pirates, as a matter of fact, are no joking matter on

today's high seas. Each year they capture millions of dollars' worth of cargo. They have also been known to scuttle ships after plundering them. Pirates operate with top speed and efficiency, counting on the element of surprise. Once they have closed in on a vessel and succeeded in boarding it, the sparse crews that normally man container ships have little defence.

Our pirates doubtless knew exactly what we carried and had chosen to bide their time, awaiting richer game. To our concerted relief they approached no closer.

The port of Abidjan, Ivory Coast, proved to be a world-class city with impressive office and apartment complexes and fashionable shops. On the surface the city was typical of urban centres anywhere in the West. Not so far away into the country's interior, however, our teams came upon a strikingly different scenario: villages of mud and thatch huts whose inhabitants roasted rats and even cockroaches for food, and children who ran in fright because they'd never seen a white person before. Which of these was the real Africa? Both, and much more.

One thing I particularly noticed about the African culture, in contrast to my own, was its acceptance of the spirit dimension. In the West we tend to ignore or deny the spiritual realm altogether: rather like the Emperor's New Clothes, it's a topic too embarrassing for polite conversation. The average African, on the other hand, is ready and even eager to talk about spiritual issues. He believes in the existence of spirits simply because he has grown up with the evidence all around him. So while the Western church struggles with the whole concept of evil spirits, and even the Holy Spirit, the African church takes the invisible in its stride. I am convinced that is why they see so much more of the Holy Spirit's power displayed, such as in healing, than we do.

Our African brothers and sisters also taught us a lot about uninhibited joy in the Lord. Ladies' and pastors' meetings on board rocked the boat, with men and women waving white handkerchiefs and swaying in praise to their creator. It was impossible not to be caught up in the general enthusiasm.

We particularly enjoyed the couple of weeks we were tied up in Ghana. Ghanaians are advocates of the maxim, 'It pays to advertise'. Everywhere we looked we were inspired by signs brightly painted with names such as: 'GOD WILL PROVIDE CHOP HOUSE', 'KING OF KINGS BUS SERVICE', 'GOD FIRST IRON WORKS', and 'GOD IS MERCIFUL HAIRDRESSING SALON'. One Sunday as we waited for our ride to church, over an hour overdue, our impatience was defused by the admonition emblazoned on a passing truck: 'DON'T DESPAIR!'

Having been involved in prison ministry in the United States I had been hoping for an opportunity to take part in Captain Isaacson's prison teams. In Ghana the captain finally allowed me to tag along with a group he was leading to a facility about ninety minutes' ride from Tema. This prison was clean and well run and received the crew's visit enthusiastically. A healthy number of believers were already attending a Bible study established through the SIM mission. That day, as inmates listened to the witness of *Doulos* men who had themselves emerged from the black hole of unbelief, several others came to a turning point.

As we were leaving we learned of a women's section to the prison and asked if we could speak there as well. It turned out that the warden was herself a Christian. She was delighted to grant permission for a programme. As the only female in our group I was elected to give the message through a Twi translator. The Lord's love became real to the women through that simple meeting, and nine opened their heart in faith.

The upsetting part was that we didn't have any literature at all in the Twi language to leave with these fledgling believers. Very few Twi Scriptures were even in print. We could only hope the warden and inmates who were already believers and owned Bibles would share them.

After lunch with SIM missionaries we made our last call, at a bleak and forbidding maximum security prison in Accra. The prisoners here were far more neglected in appearance, their clothing in poor condition, yet they jammed into the meeting room and listened intently. Mats Johannson, our Swedish bosun, was not the type to be intimidated. He knew he had a message they badly needed to hear, and if his seaman's language was plain, it also spoke to the heart.

Following the programme one of the prisoners responded with a dignified speech of thanks to the crew. A missionary later informed us that this individual was the former Vice President of Ghana. He had been ousted in a coup some years before and held 'on ice' ever since.

The prison meetings our *Doulos* teams held in Africa had a profound effect on us all. Probably the worst conditions we observed were in the Central Prison in Douala, Cameroon, where some eight thousand souls were locked away. This nightmarish place was so overcrowded that the only shelter for some men were dilapidated lean-tos they themselves patched together. These afforded little protection during the rainy season, however. Taken together with meagre food rations and a sewage system of open trenches, sickness and death were endemic.

It seemed impossible that in the midst of such dehumanising conditions there could be any hope. Yet we saw it, not only in Douala but in every other prison we visited: the unmistakable glow on the faces of those who had groped through the darkness and found the Light of the World.

The words of 'A Prison Song' written by Jeanne Guyon centuries before, came to my mind, and I realised she had expressed the truth for them all: 'But though my wing is closely bound, my heart's at liberty; My prison walls cannot control the flight, the freedom of the soul.'

6

Land of promise

*The whole Town may be considered as one
great Inn fitted up for the reception of
all comers and goers. Upon the whole there
is perhaps not a place in the known World
than can equal this in affording refreshments
of all kinds to Shipping.*

Captain James Cook
Journal, April 1771

When ship leaders first charted the course of the *Doulos*
around Africa, they wrestled with the controversial decision
of whether or not to stop in South Africa, in view of its existing
policy of apartheid. Voices were raised for and against, with
long-time supporters vehement on both sides. Finally O.M.
Ships Co-ordinator Dale Rhoton settled the issue:

If (the Apostle) Paul had determined his itinerary on
the basis of governments that measured up to certain
principles, he would have certainly bypassed the Roman
Empire with its system of slavery and other corruptions.
Indeed, on this principle our Lord would have written
off the entire planet. Our commission is to go into all
the world and preach the gospel to every creature. We
have no authority to modify our Lord's commission.

Political neutrality had always been essential to the ship's operation. Her admission into many countries hinged on it. We also knew that South Africa was weary of words. If our 'floating United Nations' was to make any impact on this troubled part of the world, it must be through a living demonstration of unity in Christ.

South Africa's media interest in our visit exceeded all expectations. Press and radio reporters haunted the ship from our first port onwards and Southwest Africa TV came aboard in Namibia for a day and a half of filming. At the same time we welcomed a crew from the South African Broadcasting Company who were planning a half-hour special on the *Doulos*. They sailed with us down to Cape Town and arranged a helicopter to take aerial footage as we came into port.

Winds were stiff and seas choppy as we neared the southern tip of the African continent, but that didn't keep us all from crowding on deck for our first stunning glimpse of the Cape. The giant mass of rock looming in front of us completely dominated the skyline. Its wide, flat summit seemed to be draped, curiously, with a 'tablecloth' of cloud. This, then, was the famous Table Mountain, and clustered at its base was the shining city of Cape Town. I think that it was in that instant that I fell in love with South Africa.

The ship was played into her berth by the lively notes of a Salvation Army brass band. A Malay choir, the Good Hope Singers, entertained the crew with a concert, and local residents in historical costume boarded to give a useful briefing on Cape Town's history. We all felt rather dazzled by the warmth of our reception.

The TV crew decided to shoot a distant view of the *Doulos* and invited me along. The vista from the top of Signal Hill gave me the sensation of standing with the world at my feet. Later a friend and I indulged in our first hamburger and milkshake in nine months and blissfully agreed we had landed on another planet.

'The streets are peaceful and sunny, no signs of violence,' I wrote to assure my parents, who imagined like the rest of the world that there was fighting on every street. 'It just goes to show how distorted our views can become when they're limited to the nightly news!'

Doulos teams that went ashore were carefully composed of mixed nationalities. We crossed colour lines repeatedly, holding meetings in white, Indian, so-called coloured and black sectors of the area. And although we were often cautioned about the risks we were taking, we saw God defuse sensitive situations again and again.

One of my teams decided to try to hold an open-air programme in a black township. At the checkpoint a guard with the South African Defense Force told us flatly that no whites were allowed inside. We explained our mission but again he shook his head. Authorities were expecting trouble in the township that day, he insisted. Finally he agreed to let us wait for a military escort.

We pulled our van over to the side and prayed. We did not want an escort. The presence of armed SADF soldiers would hardly, we felt, contribute to a relaxed atmosphere. God must have agreed with our prayers, because a few minutes later the guard came over to tell us that we were free to proceed alone, at our own risk.

We found a central spot, set up our sketchboard and began to sing. The crowd that gathered was at first silent and suspicious, but little by little, as crew members shared their personal testimony of God's love, the atmosphere thawed. Listeners began to respond, smiling and clapping; some had tears in their eyes. After the open air a good number of men and women lingered to talk or pray with us further. When we parted – with hugs and hearty handshakes – we knew we'd accomplished what we hoped for.

A team holding a programme outdoors in the centre of a high crime area called Hanover Park were disappointed when only a few spectators turned up. But next morning, when they called door to door in an apartment building overlooking the site, they met a total of fifteen people, including one entire family, all ready to confess Christ as Lord. They admitted they had been too afraid to go outside the previous evening. So they had listened – and believed – at their windows!

Doulos men and women also canvassed the Malay quarter of Cape Town, which is mostly Muslim. In an attempt to stimulate interest the team decided to hold a mini-international concert in the local school auditorium. On the advertised night I accompanied the performers to the hall. We found a total audience of about two dozen occupying the back rows. Halfway through the concert the Muslim call to prayer distracted everyone and the back row crowd got up and left. Shortly afterwards we heard people shouting and hurling stones at the school windows and roof, a decidedly nasty turn of events.

Determined not to be intimidated, we regrouped to sing and commit the situation to God. When someone pitched a stink bomb into the auditorium, however, we voted unanimously to move on. I was not keen to walk through the excited mob, but although stones continued to rain around us, none of us were injured.

All hopes of making a quick getaway died as we reached the vans: the air had been let out of several tyres. While the men of our party set about correcting the situation, we women, I'm ashamed to admit, cowered inside and prayed. Thanks to our merciful God, we were eventually able to pull away without further incident. But the encounter shook us up. It isn't pleasant to be on the receiving end of raw hatred, and we had learned a hard lesson: that discrimination can work two ways. Threats to several of our former-Muslim crew members in subsequent weeks reinforced the point.

Meanwhile, the stream of journalists and radio people never seemed to dry up. Since the resulting publicity always brought a fresh surge of visitors, no one could complain, but the task of arranging interviews with the captain and crew members did not always make me popular. All too often after the captain went to the trouble of changing into a fresh uniform or a family cleaned its cabin, the interviewer failed to show up. However, on the *Doulos* we learned to be flexible.

Among our media visitors in Durban, our last South African

port, was the lady editor of a government magazine. Lesley Dellatolla was a committed Christian who took such genuine interest in the work of the *Doulos* that it was a pleasure to show her around. When she was introduced, Susie obligingly produced some extra slides for the feature Lesley wanted to write. We parted in friendship.

Two weeks later O.M.'s South African Director, Francois Vosloo, called Susie and I into his office. The government of South Africa, he announced, had just invited the pair of us to see a bit more of the country. If we were agreeable, we could catch a commercial flight to Johannesburg that evening. The Department of Foreign Affairs would pay all expenses. The news nearly blew us away. *Lesley*, we decided. Somehow our journalist acquaintance had worked this miracle! But how could Susie and I just drop everything and leave?

In the end everyone on the ship agreed it was an opportunity simply too good to miss. Friends volunteered to take over our most urgent responsibilities. We hurriedly packed, and at 6 p.m. Susie and I were on our way to the Durban airport for the hour-long flight to Johannesburg. A taxi was waiting at the other end to transport us to the Carlton Hotel where we were to spend the first night.

We felt like a pair of Cinderellas. While Susie wandered down to the lounge for coffee I luxuriated in a bathtub (not standard equipment on the ship) and then slipped between silky sheets. The silence was blissful. No throb of generators, no loud voices . . . I fell deeply asleep, not to awaken until Susie burst into the room with a porter around midnight. She had forgotten the key.

The next morning, after stowing away an indelicate amount of breakfast, we met our assigned hostess, who was waiting outside with a swanky government car. No doubt the lady wondered how such an unimpressive pair as ourselves had been targeted for the red carpet treatment. She hid her amazement well, however, and proceeded to run through the proposed four-day schedule: a tour of two black townships, interviews with various important officials, and a day and a half inside Kruger National Park.

My eyes opened wide. *Kruger!* Visiting a natural game reserve had always been my special dream.

Susie and I responded enthusiastically, knowing too little to suggest anything else. In actual fact we were nervous. What did the government hope to gain from us, two unknown representatives of a Christian ship?

Our first excursion took us to a large training hospital in Soweto. The chief administrator himself conducted our tour through the modern and impressive complex, which included a nurses' training centre with over a thousand black women enrolled free. In one of the maternity wards of the hospital we were allowed to meet a mother with ten-day-old Siamese twins, joined at the head. Months after seeing them I read about the successful surgery that separated the infants.

After viewing a few more educational and health projects in the township we were driven to Pretoria to register at another four-star hotel. We dined that evening in the apartment of our journalistic fairy godmother. Lesley explained that when she discovered that her own department, the Bureau of Information, lacked the funds to issue an invitation to us, she had applied to the Department of Foreign Affairs. She was as delighted as we were when they accepted her proposal. After making sure we were kitted out with mosquito repellent and malaria tablets for the upcoming safari weekend, Lesley drove us back to the hotel. If this was a dream we never wanted to wake up.

Early on Friday morning we set off for the northern national state of Kangwane. Road construction made us late for an elaborate luncheon arranged in our honour with no fewer than three state officials: the Ministers of Justice, Public Works, and the Interior. Susie and I tried our best to look professional but we were in way over our heads, and we knew it. Following lunch we inspected sugar cane and coffee growing projects that were purportedly boosting the economy. More propaganda, of course, but Susie and I were learning fast.

We reached the gates of Kruger Park by early evening. Almost at once we were in another world. Impala grazed by the roadside, a great herd of black buffaloes stood with brooding dignity beside a water hole. A current of joy ran through me. 'This is your kingdom, Father!' I thought, 'all of these wonderful creatures are yours!' And I'm sure he whispered back: 'They are yours, too, child. All mine is yours.'

Eager not to miss anything, my eyes searched the brush all the way to the campground. Skukuza was only one of several accommodation sites located inside the 8,400 square mile reserve. Beds were usually fully booked at least eight months in advance, but we were told a few of the specially-built 'huts' were always kept in reserve for VIP guests. Susie and I exchanged mirthful glances. VIPs – *us*? We had by now acquired two female escorts. They took over one of the modest but comfortable round huts, and we were assigned the other.

The next morning found us climbing into the head park ranger's Land-Rover at 6 a.m. Most visitors were left to explore by themselves, so we felt highly privileged to have an expert guide at our disposal. Johann proved to be a bottomless mine of interesting information. He was always the first to spot wildlife camouflaged by the greenery, and gave us generous access to his binoculars – no small advantage.

We drove through Kruger for the entire day and for me it was Christmas, my birthday, and the Fourth of July all rolled into one. I have always been passionate about animals and there could be no greater pleasure in the world than to see them running free, in their natural habitat.

Our guide had warned us earlier that the extreme heat usually drove animals into the shade during the day, so visitors couldn't often see a great many. Susie and I, however, were sure that God hadn't brought us all of these thousands of miles without meaning to show us the variety of his creation. Sure enough, a cloud cover kept the temperature down and the animals stayed out all day. Our escorts assured us that tourists could spend a week in the park without seeing all that we did: buffalo and wildebeest, zebras, hyenas, wart hogs, baboons and wild dogs, hippos, crocodiles, giraffes and elephants, colourful birds and all types of foliage.

By late afternoon we still hadn't spotted any of the big cats, and I thought, 'Lord, you've already shown us so much, if we don't see any cats it's OK. I don't want to be greedy . . . But, God,' I couldn't help adding, 'that really would be the icing on the cake!'

Almost at once we came across three cheetahs taking a stroll down the road in front of our jeep. A few minutes later we spotted a leopard slipping into the forest. Even the ranger was impressed.

Rounding off that unforgettable day in the wild was a feast featuring thick buffalo steaks at Skukuza's posh railroad car restaurant. Although I regretted the fact that the park's buffalo population had to be limited by selective hunting, I wouldn't have wished to pass up my first taste of that succulent meat, broiled to perfection. I only mourned that my first taste would also in all probability be my last.

The next morning we prised ourselves from sleep at 4.15 a.m. so that Susie could get sunrise shots. It was still dark as we set off in the ranger's Land-Rover; even the wild dogs beside the road had sense enough to be curled up asleep. Suddenly I seized Susie's arm: a mammoth, hulking shape had suddenly materialised against the lightening horizon directly in front of us. *An elephant!*

I gulped, waiting for Johann to slow down, but to my dismay he gunned the engine and pointed our jeep right at the beast. The elephant started to run in the opposite direction down the road. Then, quite suddenly, he stopped and swung his massive bulk around to face us. My heart skipped a beat as the ranger swerved expertly around the obstacle and speeded away. The elephant would have blocked the road for ever if Johann hadn't buzzed him off, I reassured myself. All the same, any inclination to go back to sleep was forgotten.

We stopped at the top of a hill and Susie set up her tripod. The sun was just beginning to streak above the endless miles of veldt below. Johann pointed towards the far horizon. 'The

Mozambique border lies over there. Last year about sixty thousand Mozambicans made a break for freedom, hundreds through this park. Very often they're never seen again.' I shuddered. Kruger country was both beautiful and deadly. It made few concessions for the weak.

The evening before, I remembered, Susie and I had been standing near a pond, watching the splashing of hippos, when Johann cautioned us not to stand too close to the water's edge.

'Crocodiles don't give much warning,' he explained with chilling matter-of-factness. 'They just lunge out and drag their victims underwater.'

A few hours prior to that we had stopped to examine the long, narrow track of a python across the dirt road in front of us. That track, I thought, was as close to any snake as I ever hoped to get.

The sun blazed unclouded that second day and we sighted comparatively few animals before it was time to leave for the seven-hour drive back to Pretoria. But we were content.

Monday was our last day as the government's guests, and we spent it mostly in interviews with officials in the black township of Mamelodi. Lesley also gave us some more of her time, showing us through her offices in the Bureau of Information.

On our way to the airport that evening a violent thunderstorm broke. We sat for a long while in our aeroplane watching the lightning dance at the end of the runway. By the time we finally touched down in Durban and reached our floating home once more we were exhausted, more than a little dazed, and immensely happy. Our fairy-tale adventure was over, but it would remain a cherished memory for the rest of our lives.

Christmas followed on the heels of our return. This was my first shipboard Christmas, and it was enchanting to see our 'grand old lady' trimmed in red and green from bow to stern. Home-made cards and gifts appeared on cabin doors and garlands festooned the alleyways. The galley staff outdid themselves, producing a roast turkey dinner complete with

Christmas pudding. Although there wasn't one of us who didn't miss being with family and friends back home, just knowing we were 'all in the same boat' with God's family made a difference. And somehow the real Star of the day got more of the attention he deserved.

To everyone's glee an air-freighted sackful of mail arrived with perfect timing on 24 December. I hoarded most of my letters to read on deck, under South Africa's summer sun, on Christmas Day.

Why, oh why do we forget that our eagerly anticipated mail can hold unhappy surprises? As I tore open one envelope a newspaper clipping fluttered out. I scanned it and suddenly, in spite of the sun, the day turned cold. A woman and her daughter had died in the crash of a single-engine aeroplane in New England.

Nellie. I could picture her clearly: blonde and full of energy, a warm and lovely human being who had not only been my companion at work, but a friend. Her death seemed incredible. I thought of Susan, the daughter who looked so much like her, and of the shock to her surviving husband and son. The clipping was old, dated many weeks before. Somehow that made it worse.

'Oh, Nellie,' I cried silently. 'Why you? You were so young. You had so much to give.' I sat for a long time, my eyes fixed unseeingly on the horizon. There didn't seem to be any answers to plane crashes and good people dying. But perhaps, I thought at last, it was like a mystery play that made you wait for the epilogue to make everything clear. And then the characters who died during the play miraculously reappeared for the curtain call. The drama of Life that we each had a part in wasn't over yet, I told myself. I had to trust that one day, in eternity, the Author would himself tie up the loose ends that so bewildered us now. And there we would see our beloved ones once again.

The last days of my first year aboard the *Doulos* came to a close. With the entrance of the New Year we prepared for East Africa with hepatitis injections and a new course of malaria tablets.

On 6 January, sailing day, it was raining. Remembering our welcome, we should not have been surprised when over two hundred believers – black, white, and so-called coloured – arrived on the quayside despite the weather. They waited two long hours until we were cleared, singing, praying, and shouting their best wishes. We waved back furiously. Underlying our reluctance to part from these friends was a deep anxiety. What lay ahead for this lovely but troubled land?

I thought of Kevin, one of the Americans on board, who had been giving a ship tour to a group of Indians from Durban one day when he met eighteen-year-old Sean. Sean lingered to talk with Kevin, and a friendship unexpectedly flowered. After spending many hours together Sean had quietly confessed: 'I have always hated white men. You are the first white man, Kevin, that I have ever liked. I've seen Christ living in you, and I love you.'

Perhaps the dynamics of what happened between those two young men, multiplied uncountable times during the last three months, was what our ship's visit to South Africa had really been about.

A tugboat escorted the *Doulos* to the mouth of the harbour and then stood off, saluting us with three short blasts. The *Doulos* returned the courtesy and began her long voyage north, to the equator.

7

Jambo, East Africa!

*Islam is a spiritual, social, and political
force which cannot be ignored in any assessment
of issues in modern Africa.*

> J. Spencer Trimingham, 'Islam in
> Africa', *Africa Handbook*

Seven days and eight nights on the jewel-blue Indian Ocean
with no company but flying fish, dolphins and whales, were
just what we needed. The sail gave us a breathing space, a
chance to renew ourselves physically and spiritually before
reaching the very different world of East Africa.

As we reached Mombasa the early morning sun was already
dazzling. Kenya lies directly on the equator, and January is
the hottest and driest time of year. Our berth was the same
one the *Logos* had occupied ten years earlier – a prime location
right beside the busy ferry terminal. On the way, gliding past
the Youth With A Mission base, we heard singing. Early as
it was, our brothers and sisters from the mission were on the
beach, giving us their own special welcome.

The first Saturday in port was declared 'Good News Day'.
A hundred and thirty crew members and local volunteers hit
the roads with shoulder bags stuffed with English and Swahili
tracts and New Testaments. The grit and sand that stung our
eyes and sifted on to our clothing reminded us of our first
African ports. So did the eager acceptance of literature even
though this, too, was Muslim territory. We also ran across a

lot of tourists, stopping off for a tan on Mombasa's beaches after visiting Nairobi's game parks.

The 'Good Books for Africa' programme was set up once more and visitors to the exhibition carried away thousands of quality used books. Although they sold for only pennies each, their sales amounted to 20-25 per cent of our income. It was great to welcome turbanned Sikhs, black-veiled women and white-robed Muslims to the exhibition and see them occasionally buying a Christian title. Gospel Recording cassettes with music and messages in tribal languages were also popular.

Free film shows consistently attracted large crowds every night. The *Jesus* film was shown in both Swahili and English and a total of over two hundred people indicated a desire to know Jesus Christ after watching it. A team that travelled to an inland town showed the film to an open-air crowd of a thousand – and everyone remained afterwards to listen to a forty-minute message!

One sixteen-year-old boy wrote in a note of thanks: 'The cinema I attended last night made me believe and have faith in Jesus Christ. I shed tears at the sad ending of Christ who was sent to save all mankind. Some people sitting next to me laughed at me when they saw my tears. I have listened to the word of God many years but I was never a true Christian. I hope the *Doulos* crew will pray hard for me to be strong.'

Each Sunday, off-duty crew members participated in local church services. Since cars were a luxury in East Africa most of us travelled to church by *matatus* – public vans. On one trip I counted twenty-two passengers jammed into our vehicle. The team had to be peeled out when we got to our destination, a humble concrete building with a corrugated metal roof.

Sunday School was already in full swing as we sat down. To our horror we heard the young man in charge announce, 'Our sister will explain to us about the fruit of the Spirit and our brothers about the Resurrection'. I was the only sister on the team. I eyeballed our leader in panic but, fortunately, someone in the class had a question that consumed the rest of the time.

The main service was conducted mostly in Swahili. We were handed small Swahili songbooks and tried to stumble along the best we could. Africans enjoy singing so it went on for a very long time, accompanied by drums, tambourines and clapping. The first tune was 'O Come All Ye Faithful'. I noticed that worn tinsel garlands from Christmas still festooned the pulpit and front table. Also decorating the table were a bouquet of wax flowers and a flag set containing a Christian, an American, and, strangely enough, a Confederate flag.

The small sanctuary was full to bursting and stiflingly hot with the press of about a hundred adults and a hundred children. A small wireless public address system occasionally issued loud screeches. By the time Jim, our leader, got up to speak most of the allotted time was gone, so he kept his message brief. It was just as well. The translator was having a struggle understanding Jim's Australian English.

At the Writers' Workshop I held in Mombasa I met two Africa Inland Missionaries, Clarence and Marjorie Bainbridge, who taught at the nearby Pwani Bible Institute. The Bainbridges had worked in Kenya for thirty-four years. I felt it a great privilege to listen to some of their stories. We became friends and they invited me to their home and took me around some of the local sights.

With the arrival of two containers of food supplies, every able-bodied crew member was needed to form a chain that wound from the quayside up the gangways, along the decks and down to the holds. Tinned tomatoes, spinach, cheese, frozen meats and fish, big boxes of oil, salt, sugar . . . all were passed from hand to hand and stowed away, enough to keep us going through India.

On our day of departure for Tanzania we were served apples at lunch. I thought of the Bainbridges, who had mentioned once that they hadn't tasted an apple for over a year. I decided to save the piece of fruit and persuaded several shipmates to save theirs. When Marjorie and Clarence came to the quayside to see us off, we tossed down our 'thanks offerings'. The delighted surprise on their faces was more than worth our small sacrifice.

During our last week in Kenya the Tanzania line-up team had sent the ship an SOS for prayer. The berth that we wanted in Dar-es-Salaam, closest to the city centre, was occupied by a grain ship that wouldn't finish unloading for many days. The only other berth available was remotely located and unsafe for visitors.

God answered our requests for his intervention. The skipper of the grain ship obligingly moved his vessel down the quayside far enough to allow us a berth. On top of that, the port authorities reduced our fees by half! A further answer to prayer came on the very last evening in Mombasa: an overdue shipment of Indian language Bibles from the Bible Society turned up on the quayside. Meanwhile in Dar-es-Salaam, a container loaded with 40,000 Swahili Scriptures that we had ordered arrived with perfect timing from Hong Kong. All coincidence? We didn't think so.

Tanzania's Minister of Justice gave us an official welcome to the capital on 4 February. And – just in case we had any doubt about the country's religious orientation – the impressively robed ambassador of Iran presented the ship with a Koran, on behalf of the Ayatollah Khomeini!

Seven groups of crew members left the ship for a week of evangelistic outreach in other parts of the country. Four men undertook a rough, eight-hour boat trip to the island of Zanzibar to set up a mini book exhibition. Although the island is dominated by Arabic Muslims, about $1,000-worth of books were sold in only four days. A young Islamic teacher challenged the team to a public debate. He grew to like leader Mike Hack so much, however, that he called off the debate and instead gave Mike two hours to say whatever he wanted to his four hundred students.

Another team took to the air with Missionary Aviation Fellowship. They hopped to three different towns near the Mozambique border and were able to pioneer new areas for missionaries to follow up as they spoke in schools, hospitals, and in the open air.

I had been feeling a little disconsolate because I had been unable, because of my duties, to go along with any of the week-long teams. But God had something else for me. I was asked one day to act as Master of Ceremonies at a programme for ambulatory patients in the city's largest hospital. At the conclusion of our presentation, I invited those who were interested in learning more about Jesus Christ to move to one side of the room while the rest of the audience left. To our astonishment almost everyone present got up and moved to one side, en masse! We distributed the Swahili *Bridge to Life* tract, then took seventy men and women through it step by step. I was deeply moved when, at the end, they voluntarily bowed their heads and opened their hearts to the Saviour. I wouldn't have traded that moment for all of Kilimanjaro.

On the morning we were due to leave Dar-es-Salaam we discovered two stowaways under one of the book exhibition tables, about ten years old. The children had probably hidden there the night before. Following the lead of other ships we anchored once again after leaving the harbour to conduct a final stowaway search.

After ten months circumnavigating the vast continent of Africa it was time to say *kwaheri* – goodbye. The *Doulos* had welcomed well over half a million Africans up her gangways in sixteen different ports. Twenty thousand individuals on shore and on board had signed a decision to follow Christ that churches would follow up. And we had scattered lots of precious seed: half a million Christian books and Bibles plus one million tracts.

As for the men and women of the *Doulos*, the Africa experience had opened our eyes, and seared our hearts. We would never be the same.

8

Passage to India

This is indeed India! The land of dreams and romance, of fabulous wealth and fabulous poverty, of splendour and rags . . . the country of a hundred nations and a hundred tongues, of a thousand religions and two million gods, cradle of the human race, the one land that all men desire to see, and having seen once, even by a glimpse, would not give that glimpse for all the shows of all the rest of the globe combined.

Mark Twain, *More Tramps Abroad*

We left for India hoping to break our journey briefly in the Seychelle Islands. To the disappointment of all (particularly those who felt a call to tropical island paradises), our representatives in the Seychelles failed to secure permission for on-board programmes or bookselling. Our plans had to be jettisoned.

With time to spare, the good ship *Doulos* chugged along the placid waters of the Indian Ocean at a comfortable ten or eleven knots. At sea or not, we all had our regular duties to perform. Some of the book exhibition staff were transferred to the deck crew for the duration of the voyage and initiated into the joys of chipping paint, painting, or cleaning the bilges. The accommodation department set themselves the ambitious goal of cleaning every carpet on the vessel.

Every day presented a fresh challenge in finding a way back to one's cabin.

Even so, most of us were able to squeeze in a few hours on the sun-washed decks, enjoying the sight of flying fish that skimmed over the water like small silver birds. The sunrises and sunsets furnished nature's own fireworks display. And what better place than a deck at sea for a clear study of the heavens? Leaning against the rail, watching the phosphorescent gleam of our wake and stars that flashed like diamonds against the velvet throat of night, I felt sublimely content.

Just after crossing the equator the captain stopped the engines for about thirty hours. Even at our leisurely pace we would reach Bombay too early for our assigned berth. To while away the time members of the crew tried their hand at fishing, and one man managed to spear a dolphin fish (not to be confused with a dolphin) about three feet long. The galley served it up at supper that evening in bite-sized morsels. It was superb.

One calm black night when we were under way, the watchman spotted a mysterious light low on the water. The officer on duty ordered the ship off course to investigate. Could it possibly be a life raft, we wondered, drifting here in the middle of nowhere? I joined the others leaning over the rail, searching the dark swells for signs of life. But it wasn't a raft at all – only a lantern attached to a post on a small floating platform. We speculated whether the device was part of a smuggling operation or some sort of military manoeuvre. The chief officer suspected the former. To the indignation of all, however, he refused to haul up the float for a closer look and ordered the ship back on course. I was convinced we had just passed by the biggest drug find of the century.

On the second day of March we came on deck to find the outline of a great city just visible through the early morning haze. *Bombay*, Gateway to India! The excitement that flashed through the ship was not unmixed with trepidation. To most of us, India was a vast unknown.

In actual fact I hadn't wanted to land on the subcontinent

at all. Thanks to well-meant mission appeals I'd been exposed to all my life, I already had a gruesome black and white image of it fixed in my brain. Africa had been overwhelming enough, in terms of poverty, but I was certain India would be worse. O.M. India, however, had particularly requested the services of the ship's photographer and writer for producing some new audiovisual materials. It seemed unreasonable to refuse.

As it turned out, Susie and I had time to form only the briefest impressions of Bombay before we were despatched to the other side of the country. O.M. India needed a slide presentation about its women's work. They proposed that we spend a week with a girls' team in the north-east, near Calcutta; then later on, as the ship moved south, we were to link up with a second team in the state of Kerala.

Buying train tickets furnished Susie and I with our first lesson in how not to survive the subcontinent. The train station was a vast, howling cyclone of noise, people, and unintelligible announcements. Contrary to what we'd been assured, we couldn't locate anyone who spoke English. Finally, to our relief, an efficient looking individual who we took to be a railway official kindly offered to purchase our tickets for us. We stood waiting for nearly an hour before the ghastly truth finally penetrated. We had seen the last of our friendly 'official' and our precious rupees, for ever!

That was only the beginning. Blessed with total ignorance about travel in the subcontinent, my sidekick and I both naively anticipated that the Bombay to Calcutta 'Gitanjali Express' would provide a relaxing and entertaining thirty hours. A suggestion that we purchase air conditioned first class tickets was rejected with appropriate scorn. Why pay *600 rupees*, when second class was less than a third of the price?

By the first afternoon our compartment had turned into a sauna: it felt as though every drop of moisture had been sucked from our bodies. Throwing open the window only made it worse. The air outside was like a blast furnace, blowing in clouds of dust that immediately caked every inch of skin and clothing. The middle-aged couple seated opposite begged us to keep it shut.

Determined to look on the bright side, I reminded myself that dehydration would mean fewer trips to the WC. This rather spartan facility consisted of a hole in the floor, leading directly to the track below. If keeping one's seat in the madly swaying train was a challenge, keeping one's feet in the WC at the critical moment required an agility far beyond my capabilities.

Having been warned that this sort of sanitary arrangement is fairly standard in India, the prospect of a whole week on a girls' team did not entice me. It wasn't just the lack of hardware that was hard to handle, but the probable lack of toilet paper. In most of the country, tissue is regarded as superfluous when one has the use of water. Paper could even clog up the system.

I knew from our adventures in Africa that Susie was seldom bothered by such cross-cultural details. I admired her for it; nevertheless I laid in a good supply of toilet tissue in my carryall. I was also thankful that we'd thought to bring a quart of ship water and a few sandwiches and oranges to sustain us. The couple facing us were very kind and continually urged us to share their elaborate, heavily spiced meals, but we survived mainly on bottled Cold Spot soda or *chai* (sweetened milk tea). The *chai* sellers came through the compartments regularly with their big kettles and glasses, and we decided anything boiled should be safe enough to drink. That was before we took a good look at the glasses.

The hours crawled by, with the passing landscape offering little variation. Flat, arid plains gave way to occasional rice fields and tiny mud-brick villages. Here and there farmers ploughed with oxen, as their fathers before them must have done for hundreds of years.

Whenever we stopped at a station the nodding platform vendors, like wind-up dolls, scuttled into frenzied activity. So did the beggars. Ragged children crowded up to the windows, bowls extended for *baksheesh*. Others – lepers, the blind and maimed – actually boarded the train and went from compartment to compartment, exhibiting their handicaps and pleading for alms.

Susie and I were devastated. The parade of pain and poverty was something we were to face wherever we went, and we never got used to it. Eventually we learned that many beggars, especially children, are 'employed' by gang leaders and required to hand over all they collect. Such beggars generally refused to accept the food we sometimes offered in place of money. But with three hundred million people – almost one-third of India's population – living in destitution, there are all too many cases of genuine need.

Women travelling on overnight trains had the option of two different sleeping arrangements. Mixed carriages are unenclosed and thus have more traffic passing through. Ladies only compartments are partitioned and lockable, offering more protection, but they are also generally crowded and noisy since mothers usually travel with a collection of screaming offspring. Susie and I had elected to take our chances in a mixed compartment.

The sleeping berths are simple wooden or metal shelves, folded down from the wall in tiers of three. We had, unfortunately, been assigned to sleep on the lower two shelves, which left us highly vulnerable to thieves. We did the best we could, however, securing money and passports inside our clothing and sprawling on top of our possessions. Mercifully the temperature dropped after sunset, but whenever we managed to doze off the train jerked to a stop and the mosquitos descended. It was a long night.

The Gitanjali Express arrived at Howrah Station in Calcutta on the afternoon of the second day. We disembarked into nightmarish chaos. Throngs of people rushed away in every direction, porters aggressively seized our luggage, destitutes camped out in every available space. An old woman tugged at our clothes beseechingly. When I looked down I saw that she had no legs below the knee. Another beggar held out arms without hands.

As the only foreigners in sight, Susie and I attracted a good deal of attention. Men stood around us and simply stared. Since we had been advised that respectable women do not look at and certainly do not smile at strange men, it was an uncomfortable situation. When no one from the girls' team appeared, we telephoned an O.M. contact and they came to our rescue.

Oh, Calcutta! Who hasn't heard of this amazing metropolis, and imagined what it must be like? I had read Dominique Lapierre's book *City of Joy* by way of preparation but now, confronting the reality of the place, I realised that nothing could have prepared me adequately. Strange and desperate sights, smells and sounds filled my senses to overflowing. I didn't know whether to laugh or cry.

Outside the station our car became part of an impossible traffic jam eight 'lanes' wide, every vehicle trying to force a passage through the bottleneck of Howrah Bridge. It was easy to believe that an average of two million vehicles cross this stretch every day. I stifled little shrieks of alarm as we scraped dexterously between buses, taxis, trucks, animal carts and rickshaws. Even so, we were held up for so long we ended up accepting the gracious hospitality of our friends for the night. What a comfort to wash away the layers of grime at last, and sleep in quietness! The next morning we travelled on to the town where the girls were staying, about an hour outside Calcutta.

Batanagar was a factory community, built around a huge Bata shoe manufacturing complex. The eleven girls on the team were sharing the humble home of a Christian factory worker. Although the house contained only three rooms, the family had been delighted to offer one of them to the girls. This ten-by-twelve foot room served for all of the team's living, sleeping, and eating activities. Primitive kitchen and toilet facilities were shared with the family.

Under these conditions one wouldn't have expected the girls to welcome two new additions with open arms, even for a few days, so their expressions of pleasure were humbling. Especially as they were obviously still recovering from the trauma of an accident that had occurred only a few days before. One of the girls had been preparing breakfast on a tiny kerosene stove when the flame suddenly caught the edge of her nightdress and raced up her back. She was rushed to the hospital with severe burns. One or two of the other women were now staying near the hospital to look after her, as meals had to be brought in daily by family or friends.

Nine of the eleven team members in Batanagar were originally from scattered parts of India; one girl was Irish, another Argentinian. These last two belonged to Operation Mobilisation's unique Eastward Bound programme (now redesignated Asia Challenge Teams), which offered Western young people an opportunity to get close to the Indian culture. Participants at that time lived in the subcontinent for two years, spending some months in Nepal, Bangladesh or Pakistan as well. Most men and women considered it the experience of a lifetime, and found themselves at the finish with a new set of values.

I myself was already finding it easy to love the Indian people. Though very few owned possessions the Western world would consider essential to happiness, I was struck by their spirit of contentment. Indians were also ready to share the little that they did have with an open-heartedness that would put most of us to shame.

The girls on the team were at first shy, but as our newness wore off they became as playful and affectionate as kittens. The chief complaint of the Eastward Bound girls, in fact, was that their team-mates never saw the need to give them any privacy!

During our week in Batanagar we interviewed members of the team individually and photographed as much daily life as possible, setting out with them each morning to nearby villages. The houses we saw in rural West Bengal were mostly of clay, and we often found women outdoors tending clay ovens. The significance of a women's ministry in India began to dawn on me as I realised that no one but a female would ever be allowed to approach another female. The women we talked to always seemed very friendly and receptive to the literature we offered, even though shrines for idol worship were conspicuous everywhere.

Small, stagnant-looking ponds fronted some of the houses. To my dismay we often saw residents washing out cooking pots, brushing their teeth, bathing and drinking from the same source. Daily bathing is ceremonially important to Indians and they will use whatever water is available to them, but it is little wonder that life expectancy is so comparatively short.

How do you keep clothes and bodies clean without benefit of washing machines? Cleanliness in the tropics is a never-ending battle. For us on the team as well as most of the population, a bucket of cold water had to suffice for both laundry and personal bathing. Fortunately, clothes dry almost as soon as they are pegged on the line.

Water assumes an importance in tropical countries that the West cannot begin to appreciate. The simple act of drawing pure drinking water from a tap is a luxury that does not belong to three out of four people on our planet. In India I knew what it was to feel thirsty almost constantly. Cold drinks were sometimes available, but they did not have the power to quench thirst. Before any water could be drunk, however, even in a restaurant, it had to be thoroughly boiled or treated. On the team we didn't have refrigeration, so it was usually boiled and drunk lukewarm.

The purification tablets I had brought from the ship didn't turn out to be much of an asset. The first time I dropped one into a glass of water, in a restaurant, I drummed my fingers impatiently for the required ten minutes and then seized the glass and gulped it down. To my horror, the tablet was still sitting at the bottom of the glass, undissolved! Fortunately no stomach cramps materialised, so my guardian angel must have been on the job. Even after once or twice drinking from the team's untreated water jug by mistake, I had no problems. On subsequent trips I wasn't always so fortunate.

The team ate their meals in their living quarters, sitting cross-legged on the floor mat. Following their example, I learned to use my fingers to select food for my plate from platters in the centre. Susie consumed everything in front of her with great gusto. My digestive system was happier with blander fare and in the end I found it safer to stick with eggs, fruit and the flat, circular bread served with every meal, called *chapattis*.

The appearance of foreigners always caused a great sensation in the villages we visited, especially when Susie produced her camera. More than one lady Susie wanted to photograph insisted on dashing inside to change her sari. The gathering band of children on our trail made us feel like Pied Pipers.

Elections were soon to be held in West Bengal and the Communist hammer and sickle was much in evidence. Supporters periodically marched through the streets shouting propaganda through megaphones. Once members of the party stopped our little procession to advise us in no uncertain terms that there wasn't room for both our groups in the area. We went quietly, thankful to be let off so lightly amidst the volatile, pre-election fever.

During the afternoons, while the heat was most intense, the team took care of personal chores, letter-writing, and study. Those who join O.M. India for two years acquire many 'hands on' skills, but they are also required to complete an intensive Bible study programme. For most men and women, this is the only Bible school they will attend. Over the past twenty-five years virtually thousands of O.M. graduates in India have gone on to take leadership roles in their churches and communities.

The team spent the cooler evenings in Bible studies with local Christians, or in literature distribution. At least one girl on every team was a trained projectionist, so sometimes they set up an open-air movie theatre, with a sheet serving as the screen. As in Africa, the audiences that gathered for these Christian films easily numbered two or three hundred at each showing.

When it was time to turn in, Susie squeezed her bedroll among the closely packed bodies covering the team's quarters while another girl and I were farmed out to a next-door neighbour. To this simple family I must have appeared the nearest thing to an alien from space that they would ever encounter. They watched my every move with the greatest interest and I can only imagine what went through their minds as I removed the contact lenses from my eyes. But they were unfailingly courteous. The first morning they proudly produced a chair, scavenged from some unknown source, so that I would not need to sit on the floor to drink my tea!

We were due to catch our return train to Bombay on a Saturday evening, so Susie and I made up our minds to use all of our final day exploring Calcutta. What a kaleidoscope of impressions! Flashes of beauty and grace contrasted sharply with scenes of appalling squalor. Buildings evoking the days of the British Raj, like Prince Albert's fabulous Victoria Memorial, stood close to modern buildings of purely Indian design. And always, everywhere, one could never entirely erase the awareness of destitute men, women and children camped on the pavements.

Crossing a small downtown park we noticed a fenced off area of earth scarred with holes – burrows for animals, we supposed. As we stood there, a father and his daughter stopped to scatter food crumbs. To our horror hundreds of rats erupted. I felt sick, recalling then that feeding rats was a form of worship in Hinduism. According to the principles of reincarnation, almost any object or creature could host the souls of departed loved ones. So while the rats feasted, human beings died for want of bread on Calcutta's pavements, only a few yards away. Someone has estimated that rodents in India eat enough food each year to feed one hundred million people.

Calcutta, named for the goddess Kali, boasts a number of temples dedicated to her worship. On a street near one of the most famous of these we came upon the courtyard of a 'burning *ghat*', or place of cremation. Hindus regard ritual cremation of the dead as the only acceptable way of disposing of human remains. Since no foreigners are allowed inside the Kali Temple and Susie was anxious for pictures, she boldly asked permission to go into the courtyard of the burning *ghat*.

To my surprise and dismay we were allowed in. We were the only women in the crowd, I quickly noted; a few children were playing next to the pyres, adding to the macabre nature of the scene. For a moment we stood rooted in shock. Two bodies were burning on pallets in front of us: one blackened and smoking, with little remaining of what had once been a man or woman. These ashes would soon be committed to the Hooghly River. The other pallet was still engulfed in flames and the burning process had only just begun. My eyes fixed with horror on the feet of the corpse sticking out at the end, painted a bloody red. I could not look any further.

The gatekeeper urged us forward for a better view and Susie, always game for a better shot, complied. I was uneasy that we might be violating a sacred ceremony: the glances of some of the men were distinctly hostile. The officiating priest, however, seemed quite flattered by Susie's attention and must have told the others to back off. He was, most certainly, a commanding subject with his fiercely painted face, but I urged Susie to wrap up the photo session as soon as possible. The atmosphere was oppressive. It was time to get out.

Back on the street we were mobbed by stall vendors, many of whom were selling statues or pictures of gods. While we paused for another photo and studied the pictures on display, I noticed that between Ganesh the elephant god and Kali of the many arms was an artist's drawing of Jesus Christ. In Hinduism, the Lord Jesus is regarded only as one deity among millions. Individuals may choose to devote worship to him or any god with equal consequence.

Further down the road we came to Mother Theresa's small hospital for the destitute dying. We stepped inside to talk with one of the sisters, who offered to show us through the wards. I was deeply impressed, not only by the cool serenity of the place, but by the nursing staff's devotion to the pitiful scraps of humanity who lay waiting for death. The men and women on these pallets were probably receiving more loving care in their closing hours than they had known in a lifetime.

What made the difference between this anteroom of death and the place we had just come from? Love, I decided. Love and hope. For these Sisters of Mercy knew Jesus was not just another god among many. He was the One who could make a difference, both now and for eternity. And he was using their hands to prove it.

On this particular spring weekend Calcutta and all of India was celebrating the Holi festival. For reasons I was unable to discover, the traditional way to honour the god Holi is to throw coloured paint at one another. Susie delightedly snapped away at victims around the city dripping assorted colours while I spent much of the day looking nervously over my shoulder. The loose tunic and trouser outfit I was wearing, called a Punjabi suit, was borrowed, and I didn't want anything to happen to it. When we finally dropped into our seats on the Bombay mail train that evening, unscathed, I heaved a sigh of relief.

Alas, my relief was premature. At our first stop someone tossed a bucket of paint against the side of the train that splashed through the window, directly on to my clothes. Mercifully, the paint turned out to be the washable kind!

The return to Bombay took six hours longer than the Gitanjali Express. Susie and I were assigned separate compartments this time and I shared mine with a Muslim family. In the morning we presented an amusing picture as the couple devoted themselves to their Koran, while I sat opposite reading my Bible. It was a great pity that we couldn't communicate.

At long last we reached the end of the journey and staggered off the train, covered with grit from head to toe. Home at last! Climbing the *Doulos* gangway once more, we laughingly hailed a few of our shipmates. Their response was disappointingly half-hearted.

'Hey, what's wrong with you guys?' we demanded. 'What kind of welcome is that?'

Rhonda Adams, the *Doulos* Director's wife, was just stepping on to the deck nearby. She drew us aside.

'Welcome back girls. I'm afraid we just got some sad news.'

Rhonda told us briefly how, a few days before, one of the Korean girls had gone into the city with a friend. Prisca had stepped on to a bus and the vehicle started to pull away before her companion could get on. Prisca panicked. She jumped off and fell, striking her head sharply on the pavement.

Our shipmate had been taken to the hospital semiconscious. Later she slipped into a coma, and doctors determined that she had suffered brain damage. Prisca had died just a few hours before our return.

I was stunned. The next day, still in a state of disbelief, the ship's company left the *Doulos* – her flag lowered to half mast – and met in a nearby church. Prisca Ahn's memorial service was translated into Korean and videotaped for the benefit of her family.

'I eagerly expect and hope that I will in no way be ashamed,' we read together from the first chapter of the Book of Philippians, the twentieth and twenty-first verses: 'but will have sufficient courage so that now as always Christ will be exalted in my body, whether by life or by death. For to me, to live is Christ and to die is gain . . .'

A Christian nurse who worked in the hospital where Prisca was taken had commented: 'Every day I see people dying in here from these sort of accidents. But this one is different. She came to India only to serve us, and now this. I said, "Why her, Lord, and not me?"'

Now, with heavy hearts, we each asked ourselves the same question, knowing that it could have happened to any of us. Were we as ready as Prisca had been? We filed by to look at our sister for the last time. Prisca had been the closest of all my Korean friends. I remembered her quiet grace and joy, and it struck me that this was the only time I had seen her face without a smile. Was this really the same girl who was always so ready and eager to share her faith? I knew it wasn't. The real Prisca was laughing and alive somewhere else, in the presence of her Lord.

Back on the ship, preparations began for sailing the next day to Mangalore. I passed the small pantry in the women's section, used for making coffee and tea, and stopped. Someone had placed a few small possessions inside, with a note.

'To my sisters,' I read slowly, 'With love from Prisca.'

The words finally broke the aching dam of tears inside me. 'Goodbye, dear friend,' I whispered. 'Thank you. We will carry your love with us, always.'

9

Southern comfort

*The body travels more easily than the mind,
and until we have limbered up our imagination
we continue to think as though we had stayed
at home. We have not really budged a step
until we take up residence in someone else's
point of view.*

John Erskine, *The Complete Life*

During our two weeks in the Gateway to India nearly twenty-four thousand Indians had visited our conferences and book exhibition. It was a good start; even our sorrow had served to forge a strong bond between ourselves and local believers.

Associate Director Mike Stachura used the farewell rally to challenge Bombay Christians. Who, he asked, would take Prisca's place in service for God and offer themselves as 'living sacrifices'? Who would be willing to live and, if necessary, die for their faith? Fifteen men and women stood to pledge their solemn commitment.

Three dozen Indian O.M.ers had actually joined our crew for the next three months. Their presence on the *Doulos* would be essential in helping us bridge the culture gap.

The port of Mangalore numbered only about four hundred thousand residents compared to Bombay's ten million. In the tropical beauty of the south we began to relax – but not for long. Susie and I joined sixty other shipmates for a twelve-hour bus trip inland to 'the garden city' of Bangalore. In the city's ornate town hall the crew performed an International Music Programme for an audience of 750, which included the mayor. The following week they were involved in a number of church and school programmes, and offered a mini book exhibition.

Susie and I left Bangalore early to travel on to a girls' team further south. We couldn't resist taking a detour on the way, however, to the ancient city of Mysore. Mysore's main tourist attraction is the Amba Vilas, one of the largest and most extravagant palaces in India. Amba Vilas was built in 1897 to replace the original residence, which, it was said, was burned down by a maharajah who got tired of it. This second palace was created by Englishman Henry Irwin.

The visitor approaching the Amba Vilas for the first time will immediately notice its imposing central tower, crowned with a massive, gilded dome that can be seen for miles around. At night the entire building is outlined by some fifty thousand light bulbs. The tour of the interior also left Susie and I gasping. Amba Vilas fulfils every fairy-tale fantasy of maharajas' palaces – including marble floors, ivory wall panels, and a solid silver throne.

From the top of Mysore's Chamundi Hill visitors can enjoy an excellent view of the city. It is also the site of two gigantic statues, one of the god Shiva's bull, Nandi, which is perpetually decorated by the flowers of pilgrims; and one of the sword-wielding demon Mahishasura. Nearby is a twelfth-century temple devoted to the goddess Shri Chamundeswari, who was believed to have vanquished the demon.

The temple was open to visitors and, since I had never before been inside one, Susie and I left our sandals outside and stepped in. Our first impression was that we had plunged into a cave. A thick, impenetrable darkness closed around us, the heavy scent of incense choking our breathing. As our eyes began to focus we could make out, here and there, the images of cows, rats, cobras and other deities set into hollowed alcoves and illuminated by candles. Priests sat by some of the shrines, prepared for a small fee to celebrate *pujas* – reverential ceremonies – on the worshippers' behalf. During such rites of adoration the images might be bathed or dressed, perfumed or adorned with flowers, or offered food or drink.

'You shall have no other gods before me . . . for I, the Lord your God, am a jealous God . . .'

The words thundered through my head as loudly as though they had been spoken aloud. I shivered, feeling the same almost tangible sense of oppression that I had experienced in the burning *ghat* in Calcutta. Neither Susie nor I were inclined to linger. We collected our sandals and fled back into the sunshine.

The second girls' team we had targeted was located in the middle of soft, green countryside, about three hours outside the city of Cochin in Kerala state. It was a small team of half a dozen members, including one Eastward Bound woman from Switzerland. Although they lived very simply, they were lucky enough to have a small, unfurnished house to themselves.

As I crawled into my sleeping bag that first night, following a late open-air film show, I prayed fervently that I wouldn't have to obey any calls of nature in the next few hours. The girls had already warned me to be sure to wake someone to go with me, if I had to use the outdoor toilet. One of the team, they explained, had recently killed a cobra in the back yard. And cobras usually came in pairs!

Fortunately I escaped any nasty confrontations with snakes, although one did slide by me one day as I stood watching villagers harvest rice in the fields. The cockroaches were bad enough, ugly brutes at least two inches long. At least the roaches on our ship hadn't yet learned to fly!

I was afraid that I did not make very good missionary material. All the missionaries I had read about in books seemed to have taken such inconveniences as reptiles, insects and heat in their stride. Susie and I had exchanged the dry heat of the north for the extreme humidity of the south and the temperature was continuing to climb. Perspiration streamed from us unceasingly and I had never felt so hot in my life. To keep from dehydrating we followed the team's advice and drank coconut milk. The juice was a welcome alternative to iodine-treated water and proved surprisingly effective in slaking thirst. We also indulged in cold water bucket baths as frequently as possible. Sadly, the relief these afforded was only short-lived.

As we got better acquainted, we enjoyed seeing the distinctive personalities of each girl on the team begin to emerge. Mariamma took the prize as chatterbox, always giggling but quite earnest about the training she was receiving. Mariamma thought God might be preparing her for future evangelism in one of the more spiritually resistant northern states of India.

Annie, the team leader, was a serious girl who had suffered painfully from shyness before joining O.M. Separation from her family had been a big step, she told us, but team life had gone a long way towards helping her grow up.

The strikingly lovely features of Sunita were shadowed by a sad past. Orphaned at seven, she had grown up lonely and unwanted until, in her teens, she finally decided to put an end to her life. The girl made two unsuccessful suicide attempts and had already bought poison for a third try when she stopped to listen to a street preacher. The new life Jesus Christ offered was exactly what Sunita was looking for. She became a Christian and joined O.M. a few months later. In the mission, she said, she felt she had finally found a family.

It was an education to follow the girls through this lovely land of deep waters and quiet rivers. Like most teams, they planned to stay two or three months in one place and visit as much as possible of the surrounding area door to door.

By the end of the week Susie and I were ready to catch a ride to Cochin with an O.M. men's truck team. The young men who joined these mobile teams, we decided, had to be as rugged as the roads they travelled all over India. They didn't always enjoy a friendly reception. In a few cases men have been beaten up by extremists, their literature burned. On our particular trip we stopped twice in town centres to hold open airs, using the truck bed as a platform. The speakers used megaphones which attracted a large number of interested pedestrians, but thankfully we didn't start any riots.

Cochin was the southern command headquarters of the Indian navy and a busy commercial port. Susie and I were to rejoin the *Doulos* here when she arrived the next day. With all O.M. India accommodation already crowded to capacity, we were forced not too reluctantly to find room in the local inn. What luxury! An air-conditioned hotel complete with soft bed and Western-style toilet, all for under ten dollars for the two of us.

The next day we were all set to welcome the *M.V. Doulos* into port in style. The harbour master, who was a Christian, invited several dozen of us to cram aboard his tugboat, and we sallied out to guide her in. What a happy moment to draw close and recognise our friends at the rails, all grinning and madly snapping photos! It was good to come home.

The church of Kerala in Southern India traces its beginnings to the visit of the Apostle Thomas in AD 52. The state now has the highest percentage of Christians in the nation. It is also, interestingly enough, the most literate and prosperous state. We were taken by surprise when seventy-eight thousand visitors flocked aboard the ship. All of them received New Testaments, and the attendance at Christian conferences broke a five-year record.

One evening some of our men were kicking a football around on shore near the *Doulos* when they noticed they were being watched by sailors from a neighbouring ship. The sailors, Russian, readily accepted the proposal of a match the next night. They sealed the deal over cups of coffee on the *Doulos*, talking until quite late, and when they finally left they were clutching gifts of Russian Bibles and tracts.

The next night the football game ended in a draw. This time the Russians were ready with an invitation to their ship, where our men were invited to explain more about their faith. The Commissar himself – official political representative – obligingly volunteered as a translator!

The Russian vessel was due to pull out early the next

morning, so after they got home the *Doulos* men sat up late. At 6 a.m. they were back on the quayside, waving their friends off with a banner lettered in Russian: 'GOD LOVES YOU AND SO DO WE!'

The *Doulos* reached Madras at the end of May. It was time for me to say my own goodbyes. Susie and I had been asked to continue our adventures at sea the following September, this time aboard the *M.V. Logos*, in South America. I wanted to report first to churches back home that were supporting me.

Some of my friends have compared the confining life aboard a ship to an emotional pressure cooker. Others say it's like living in a fish bowl. Personally I am inclined to think of God's navy as a blender experience. O.M.'s ships shake nationalities and personalities together until each person adds his or her own unique flavour to enrich the whole; then we are poured out to a thirsty world. After sixteen months of shared agony and ecstasy with shipmates like Trina and Roberto, Uwe and Mabel and Prisca, I knew they would for ever be a part of me, and I of them.

10

Assignment: Andes

> *Bolivia is the Switzerland of South America, a Republic without access to the sea. In shape it resembles the hall of a great hotel, a huge green carpet at the foot of a staircase that rises to a flat landing a good deal nearer the stars. Nine-tenths of the population live either at the top or half way down . . .*
>
> Julian Duguid, *Green Hell*

Susie and I flew out to join the *Logos* in Arica, Chile, early in the autumn of 1987. Susie had served before with the *Logos*, so she at least harboured no delusions of what we were coming to. She stopped to point out our new home as we trundled our baggage past the pelicans and along the wharf.

'Look, Debbie, do you see her? Over there!'

'That's the *Logos*? That little white boat?' I burst into slightly hysterical laughter. 'You don't seriously mean 140 people live on that thing?'

She smiled. A few minutes later we were welcomed aboard as members of the crew, without even a cabin to call our own. The chief steward explained apologetically that we would have to move from cabin to cabin as their respective owners left on breaks.

The *Logos* was compact – only eighty-two metres long – but what a beauty! A royal vessel, originally commissioned by the

Danish crown, with a reception area and dining room boasting fine polished marquetry and inlaid decks. The family atmosphere of the *Logos* enfolded us instantly. She was a happy ship, and I was glad we had come to be a part of her.

Of course, the main drawback to a floating mission is that it's limited to what it can reach by water. When the *Logos* received as SOS from the churches of landlocked Bolivia, we knew we had a problem. Still, while 2,300 tons of steel may not be portable, books – and people – are. And more than anything else, the *Logos* was people.

Bolivia's evangelical community was like a pebble tossed into a vast desert of Christo-paganism. Believers felt isolated; they were desperate for contact with other believers, basic Bible teaching and practical evangelism training. They also needed more Christian literature. To my delight, Susie and I were chosen to be part of a one-week team that would take books and hold seminars in the cities of La Paz and Caranavi.

Our Aero Boliviano 727 lifted off from Arica on a brilliant October afternoon, circling high above the barren Alticama desert before heading towards the Andes. The twenty-five minute flight was a stunning introduction to the 'Switzerland of South America'. The mountain chain that separates Chile from Bolivia is mostly uninhabitable, sprawling in endless brown waves with only the tallest peaks and volcanoes dusted in white. As we neared La Paz, Lake Titicaca's brilliant blue stood out in vivid contrast to the reddish-brown patchwork of adobe farms.

The city of La Paz lies in a natural basin, rimmed by the Andes. At 12,800 feet above sea level it is the highest capital in the world, and breathtaking in every sense of the word. In fact, some new arrivals have been known to transfer directly from their planes to an oxygen tent. I personally found gasping for air a most uncomfortable sensation. Several others were also feeling the first effects of altitude sickness by the time we reached our accommodation.

Our Youth With A Mission hostess was ready to ply us

with 'a good cup of tea', however; and not just any tea. Coca tea is the standard Bolivian remedy for sickness. Natives chew leaves of the coca plant to alleviate pain or hunger, and raw cocaine was for many years the country's chief illegal export. But coca tea, our hostess assured us, was quite legal and perfectly harmless.

Although it proved unsuccessful in relieving my headache and nausea I was ready and eager the next day to set off as planned. Three of us had been asked to teach practical evangelism methods to new recruits in a newly established YWAM base over the mountains. *Logos* evangelism leader Dale Konkol, hopefully, would handle most of the instruction; this would free Susie and I to do some photography and writing on the side.

Caranavi lies some ninety miles away from La Paz and there is only one road, through the tortuous La Cumbra Pass. To reach the city by bus it takes about seven hours. The cheaper way, riding in the open back of a truck, can take as much as five hours longer. Susie voted for the truck, convinced she'd be able to shoot better pictures in the open air. Dale and I were less enthusiastic. We finally got our way by pointing out the very real possibility of a rainstorm.

The bus reminded me of the old-fashioned kind we used to ride to school. The seats were hard and upright and our knees were crushed against the seats in front. Our bags had to be stuffed under our legs or else tied on top of the roof as there was no overhead rack. But for a fare of only $3.50 one way, $4.50 on return (because it takes more petrol), who could complain?

The only other gringo on the bus turned out to be another missionary. Philip Kittleson was on his way back to the radio station he helped to maintain in Caranavi for a group called A Cup of Cold Water Ministries. His parents, he said, were also missionaries in Bolivia. Tall, bearded and genial, Philip's years in the country had given him an encyclopaedic knowledge that he wasn't shy of sharing.

As the bus left the outlying houses of La Paz behind, we

started our vertical ascent. Suddenly and without ceremony the driver stuck his arm out of the window and poured out the contents of a bottle of alcohol. A drink offering to the gods, our friend explained, grinning at our startled expressions. Many Indians – even those who became 'Christians' – still regarded the mountains as deities, he said.

By the end of the first hour we had ascended to the highest elevation of the pass, about fifteen thousand feet. Entirely encircling us were spectacular, cloud-wreathed peaks, vast snowfields and ice-water cascades. On the slopes below the snow line, scattered herds of llamas, donkeys and sheep grazed on the windswept scrub.

Zig-zag paths slashed the mountainsides. Philip told us these were used for bringing ice down from the peaks. Blocks of ice were stored in stone houses until they were transported further down. It was all part of the Andes' refrigeration system.

With an average monthly income of only $45 per capita, Bolivia is considered South America's poorest country. At the time of our visit only about 4 per cent of Bolivia's road system was paved. Philip said many stretches became impassable during the rainy season.

Rockslides also posed a constant threat. At one point our track was cut off by fallen rock and we were forced to detour around it. Wherever the road was wide enough vehicles passed us going the other way to La Paz, piled high with produce and people. We chuckled at the spectacle of one man clinging to the hood of a truck with one hand, the other clutching a container of water, ready to douse the overheated engine.

Soldiers suddenly materialised in front of us, waving the bus to a stop. Only a routine search for drugs, Philip assured us as the men boarded and glanced around. If trafficking was a major industry in these mountains I didn't wonder that such cursory inspections had done little to slow it down.

As we proceeded, the road continued to narrow until it

was little more than a crude ribbon carved in the face of the rock. Our guide drew our attention to a marker near the edge commemorating the spot where political prisoners had been thrown off the cliff in 1944. I peered down the sheer vertical drop, which was entirely too close for comfort, and shuddered.

Other monuments began to appear with depressing regularity after that: white crosses decorated with flowers commemorating the deaths of unlucky motorists. I was already feeling rather queasy when our bus driver obligingly slowed to allow passengers a good look far down the mountain at the wreckage of a pickup that had crashed the previous week.

It is odd how, at moments like these, one becomes acutely conscious of small details – like the small skeleton dangling from the bus driver's rear view mirror. Across the aisle I noticed a lady passenger inhaling deeply from a small oxygen device. Another man was devoting himself to a newspaper entitled 'La Ultima Hora' – The Last Hour. If only I could have removed my paralysed grip from the seat in front of me it would have been the chance of a lifetime to pass out tracts.

At around noon our bone-rattling conveyance braked to a halt. The rough public café was not exactly the Holiday Inn, but neither were the prices. A traveller could eat like a king for under one US dollar. Not possessing one, we settled for bread rolls and local fruit, sharing a bottle of carbonated Papaya Salvietti, the national beverage, with our Cup of Cold Water friend.

During the last half of the trip the road dipped into a luxuriant, subtropical rainforest with groves of banana trees and steeply terraced coca fields. Here and there a mountain waterfall splashed directly on to the bus. I took these occasions to remind Susie, who was still muttering darkly about not getting any decent shots, of what our fate would have been in an open truck.

Below us, in a dizzyingly distant gorge, wound the Coroico River. We tried not to notice that our tyres passed only a precarious few inches from the brink. As the bus stopped and backed for the hundredth time to allow another vehicle to scrape by, Philip volunteered the information that only a few days before, a bus like ours had slipped over the edge here.

I turned to check the back door and saw a sign which read 'No Escape'. I took it this was 'No Escape' in Spanish, but Dale assured me it only meant 'No Spitting'. A superfluous warning, I thought; my mouth was as dry as dust.

The sensation was no doubt aided by the choking clouds that were now billowing through the windows and powdering us all into ghosts. We reached a bridge that Philip told us was built in the late fifties to complete the road to Caranavi. Before that time travellers were obliged to hop on a balsam raft. I privately thought that sounded like a lot more fun.

At 5.30 p.m. we reached the end of our road. Philip hiked halfway up a mountain to his radio station and returned with his home-made jeep. We thought it was very obliging of him to cart us and our luggage to the YWAM house, which was all the way up to the summit. Our Bolivian brothers and sisters gave us a welcome that was fully as beautiful as the view.

It did not take long to realise that these young mission recruits did not suffer from materialism. Compared to the extreme simplicity of their diet and surroundings, our *Logos* lifestyle was positively luxurious. But these young men and women felt in no way deprived. Discipleship Training School was more than a temporary 'upward-bound' experience: it offered a new direction for the rest of their lives.

During the following days they soaked in every ministry technique we could come up with: how to give an effective testimony, how to perform rope trick illustrations and mime, how to paint sketchboard messages. One afternoon our students took their skills to the local plaza. The response to their open air fired them with enthusiasm.

On our second evening half a dozen of us piled into the back of a pickup truck to visit a prison farm. The truck bounced through the jungle for some time until the road abruptly ended at a river that boiled with white water. To my horror I saw that we were expected to abandon the truck and haul ourselves by a pulley over the river, two at a time, on a suspended platform.

The farm wouldn't have made anyone's model prison list. The living conditions of the inmates were better suited to animals, I thought, than men. When only a handful attended our meeting I was puzzled. Surely there wasn't too much competition in the entertainment line? But we learned afterwards that local priests were pressurising officials to discourage the visits of evangelicals. Those bold enough to come seemed grateful, and my heart stirred with compassion. If human beings ever stood in need of cheer or comfort it was these men.

It was raining and the mosquitos were biting savagely by the time we swung back over the river and headed home. I remembered the yellow fever injections we had grumbled about on the ship. Our Bolivian companions probably didn't have the advantage of such protection. Medical treatment was an unaffordable option in this part of the world, and yellow fever and tuberculosis were still major killers.

Our time in Caranavi was over too quickly. Departure day dawned heavy with rain and fog, making the pass even more treacherous than usual. But buoyed up by the loving send-off of our YWAM friends, the long trip back didn't seem to matter. We had received far more from these young people than we had been able to give.

Meanwhile, back in La Paz, our team-mates were finishing a crowded week of seminars and programmes. Most of the books we'd brought had disappeared like snowflakes in the sun. The denominational rivalries we'd heard might be a problem had never surfaced; in fact, each day a different church claimed the responsibility for furnishing the team's main meal.

On the final afternoon I took time to explore the city's central market area, Plaza San Francisco. Black-braided Indian women sat with their wares, picturesque in derby hats and colourful woven blankets. It was the kind of scene photographers die for, but I knew, even before I asked, that the women would refuse to pose for me. They were afraid. Superstition taught them that if I captured their image with my camera, I might somehow also capture their soul.

During the course of my wanderings I nearly stepped on the body of a well-dressed man, stretched senselessly on the busy pavement in front of me. Concerned, I applied to another pedestrian for help, but he only shrugged and shook his head. The man was only a *boracho*, he declared, a drunk. Why concern oneself with a drunk?

La Paz. Peace. But even a city that almost touched heaven was not exempt, it seemed, from the far-reaching influence of hell.

I was glad that the *Logos* had found a way to reach this landlocked country. God was deliberately planting his footsteps in the rugged vastness of the Andes, where they belonged as much as anywhere else. For the mountains are his, too, he had been reminding us – as much as the sea.

11

Shipwreck!

I will not doubt though all my ships at sea
Come drifting home with broken masts and sails;
I will believe the Hand which never fails
From seeming evil worketh good for me.
And though I weep because those sails are tattered,
Still will I cry, while my best hopes lie shattered,
'I trust in Thee!'

Ella Wheeler Wilcox, *Faith*

New Year's Eve, 1987. I stood on the boat deck of the *Logos* as the midnight exploded with sirens, horns and flares from shipping all over the harbour. Our little ship had reached Ushuaia, Argentina, the southernmost town in the world. Only seven hundred miles of sea separated us from Antarctica.

Over the last two months we had sailed down the whole length of Chile, putting into three more ports after Arica. In Valparaiso the President himself had come aboard. Each day we welcomed an average of three thousand visitors.

Although we had also managed to pick up a few health problems – one case of hepatitis and two of typhoid – I was enjoying South America. The Latin people were full of vitality and warmth, and many had come to recognise the need for a faith that could help them cope with everyday problems. Others had expanded their awareness of the world through the ship's visit.

At Christmas we held a special Christmas-Around-the-World celebration for the residents of Punta Arenas, on the Strait of Magellan. Now we had left Chile for this small port in Tierra del Fuego, 'Land of Fire'. Ushuaia was a startlingly beautiful settlement, lying at the foot of snow-covered mountains on the Beagle Channel. Its very remoteness meant that few ships called, so the town gave our books and family conferences an eager reception.

On 4 January 1988, we finished a short but busy programme and cast off early in the evening. Our next voyage was to take us from the Pacific to the Atlantic and the Argentinian city of Puerto Madryn. First, however, we had to pass through the Beagle Channel. The whole area was notorious for stormy weather and navigational hazards, and that very night we were headed into a Force Eight gale. The ship was already beginning to roll unpleasantly when the crew met for a brief exchange of news and prayer. Most of my friends turned in early.

I lingered on deck for as long as I could, reluctant to miss any of the stark splendour of this lonely passage. When I finally went below I took the precaution of putting my typewriter on the floor. Failure to secure it properly on the last trip had caused the poor machine to take a near-fatal nosedive. Most of the keys still functioned, but I feared they would never be quite the same.

Tomorrow, I thought as I rolled into my narrow bunk, I would have to tackle the port report – if I wasn't too seasick. Rocked by the heavy pitch and roll beneath me, I slid into deep unconsciousness.

In what seemed like only a few minutes I was jolted awake by a loud grating and scraping noise. The ship shuddered violently and books and other objects fell from my shelves. 'Must be a bad storm,' I thought groggily, pulling the blankets over my head. Then I heard voices, confusing sounds of people running and shouting in the alleyway. Finally someone pounded on my door.

'Put on your life jacket! Don't panic!'

I bolted out of bed. The hands on my clock pointed to midnight. I pulled a sweatshirt and slacks over my nightgown, then slung on an extra sweater and bulky life jacket before racing up the steps to the dining room. Everybody was gathering there – a good sign, I thought, relieved. If we were in serious trouble we'd all be heading for the boat deck.

The faces around me were tense. A few girls were sobbing quietly, but there was no panic. The ship leaders explained that the ship's bow had gone hard aground on submerged rocks. Fortunately the hull did not appear to be seriously damaged and no water was entering the ship. The deck crew was already pumping out the forward ballast tanks to lighten the bow. Since the tide was rising, there was every expectation that we could safely reverse off the rocks by dawn.

Through the next long hours we waited together, praying and singing and talking quietly. Our faith was strong. We were certain God would rescue this ship. It was his – the *Logos* had served him effectively for seventeen years. Various people shared verses of encouragement from the Psalms:

> 'From the ends of the earth I call to you, I call as my heart grows faint; lead me to the rock that is higher than I . . .' (Psalm 61:2). 'He who dwells in the shelter of the Most High will rest in the shadow of the Almighty . . .' (Psalm 91:1). 'You will not fear the terror of night, nor the arrow that flies by day, nor the pestilence that stalks in the darkness . . .' (Psalm 91:5,6). '"Because he loves me," says the Lord, "I will rescue him; I will protect him . . ."' (Psalm 91:14).

Restless, I stepped out into the windy night and picked out the comforting lights of another ship standing by. The Chilean Navy had responded to our distress call. Forward, the deck crew were taking soundings. I peered down over the bow where a spotlight illuminated the water and weedy rocks, and shuddered.

How had this thing happened to us? Later we learned that the special pilot hired to navigate the channel had left the ship prematurely. Because of the rising storm, his pilot boat had radioed the bridge with the message that they wished to return to port. The pilot was fearful that he would be stranded on the *Logos* for the whole four-day voyage. So he requested – and received – the captain's permission to disembark to his waiting launch. Exactly twelve minutes later, at 11.56 p.m., we ploughed on to the submerged reef.

The storm was now diminishing, but the waves and wind continued relentlessly to pound the ship against the rocks. The *Logos* struggled like a living thing to right herself. We believed with all our hearts that she would, but we didn't know, then, that her back was broken – that her keel bar had been snapped in two, and that her wound was mortal.

The angle of the decks was making it increasingly difficult to walk. On the foredeck I found crew members lashing the book exhibition cabinets to keep them from sliding to the port rail. I was suddenly aware of our danger. If these cabinets – or, worse, the vans we carried on the aft well deck – broke loose and slid to the port rail, we would certainly capsize.

Several decks below, a young American deckman named Brian Stan was keeping watch in the holds. It had now been determined that the ballast tanks under the lower deck had been damaged. The attempt to deballast, or pump out the water, was futile as sea water was coming in too fast. But the *Logos* was an icebreaker, and so far her sturdy double bottom had prevented the water from entering the holds.

Suddenly, just before 5 a.m., Brian heard the sound he had been dreading all night – the gush of water flooding into the ship. He grabbed the phone and reported to the bridge. Then he got out, fast.

The ship's company were ordered to assemble at the starboard rail in a last-ditch effort to check the heavy list to port.

We huddled close, trying to shield ourselves from the stinging cold. I wished desperately for a hat and gloves, but there was no chance now of returning to our cabins. The order came to report to our lifeboat stations.

Incredibly, even at this point there was still no visible panic, even from the eight small children in our company. The training of countless safety drills now came to us automatically. We helped each other slip and slide over the sharply pitched decks to our assigned stations. There we clung to whatever we could find to stay upright. It was all like a bad dream. I couldn't believe that we would actually be asked to leave our home, everything we owned.

But then, at 5.10 a.m., the captain appeared on the bridge wing above us. I saw him cup his hands over his mouth, heard him shout the words we had never imagined it possible to hear: *'Abandon ship . . . Abandon ship!'*

My boat was on the port side, Number Two. Sitting jammed together though we were, we tried our best to obey instructions to hold on to the lifelines while the boat was lowered. The rope burned our hands and then we hit the surface of the water. I looked up. The giant white hull of the *Logos* leaned over us with menace, as though she would capsize upon us any second.

'Oh, God!' I groaned fearfully. 'Help us get away!' But we seemed incapable of getting free of the lines. The oars were unshipped; they were heavy and awkward and we were clumsy, unaccustomed to handling them. I exchanged places with some girls beside me and pulled hard. With agonising slowness we half rowed, half drifted away from the *Logos*.

Within minutes another vessel roared alongside. Her wake washed over our stern, soaking us with icy water. Hands reached down and pulled us, one by one, to safety. Then we watched anxiously as a Chilean torpedo boat and tugboat completed the rescue. A muster was taken, each of us responding to our shouted names, then taken once more. We hugged each other with relief. Everyone had got off. Everyone was alive.

Someone exclaimed and we looked back. Through the

morning mist, arched over the home we had just abandoned, we could see a brilliant rainbow. It was exactly as though God was giving us his special reassurance: *Those who put their trust in me will never be disappointed.*

Officers of the Chilean Navy who watched the evacuation that morning later confessed they had expected to pick up bodies, not survivors. *Logos* decks had already reached a twenty degree angle – five degrees beyond the maximum for launching boats without a severe risk to life. Anyone who fell into the arctic channel would have perished within minutes.

Kevin Copeland of Northern Ireland, coxswain of Lifeboat Number Six, told me how his boat had been jammed in the chocks, or blocks, that held the keel: 'Five of us were forced to lift the boat manually so that it could swing out on the davits. It weighed about two and a half tons.' He added, 'In a drill just the week before, seven of us couldn't budge it!'

Boat Five, starboard aft, was being cranked down with two men inside when the violent lurching of the *Logos* caused it to swing and wedge inside a lower deck rail. The two young crew members found themselves suddenly dangling by the lifelines, trying to claw the boat back out with their feet. Two others on deck grabbed a board to pry the boat free. After a frantic interval they succeeded.

Lifeboat One's passengers included two small children. It, too, was lowered at an impossible angle and caught on a lower deck rail, tilting crazily. The lifelines saved the occupants from spilling into the water, but they were then forced to climb out of the boat while it was freed. Then they tried it again. This time the boat lowered safely past the rail, but there was imminent danger that a stream of bilge water being pumped out of the side of the ship would flood the boat. To everyone's astonishment, precisely as the lifeboat drew level with the jetting water, the engine stopped, cutting off the pump and stream of water.

With all of us safely accounted for, the two Chilean Navy ships set out for Puerto Williams, a tiny outpost several hours back down the Beagle Channel. Like others I had wet clothes and couldn't seem to stop shivering. Eventually the sailors handed out coffee, the best I ever tasted, hot and sweet. Those who were seasick shared the few bunks that were available and tried to sleep. I joined others on the floor, my eyes fixed with wonder on a small artificial tree, still decorated. Our lighthearted celebrations of Christmas, only ten days before, now seemed very remote.

In Puerto Williams the Navy assembled blankets, hot food, and places to sleep. The little community opened their homes to the families; single men and women were assigned to the community centre or schoolhouse. The isolated settlement could cover only a few of the needs of 140 unexpected refugees. We found ourselves sharing combs, towels and even toothbrushes.

Already news networks from all over the world were calling in, jamming the base's one telephone line, for details of the shipwreck. Whether I wished for it or not, I had the kind of scoop most journalists dream about. I borrowed paper and pencil, and as the girls around me settled into sleep, lulled by the comforting crackle of the schoolhouse's wood stove, I began to write.

12

The great outdoors

*For while we are in this tent, we groan
and are burdened . . .*

2 Cor. 5:4

In the end, an official Navy enquiry pronounced all parties
involved in the shipwreck free from responsibility. The *Logos*,
uninsured and 'economically unsalvageable', was turned over
to the Chilean Navy for disposal. We crew members were
airlifted first to Punta Arenas, then Buenos Aires, Argentina,
where we each had to make some hard decisions about the
future.

The churches of South America had responded dramatically
to the *Logos* disaster. As soon as it became known that we had
lost everything, used clothing began to pour into the Buenos
Aires collection point from all parts of the continent. A fund
was established to replace some of our belongings.

It was not, of course, the replaceable things that we
most mourned. If we had been given time to go back
to our cabins and rescue our most precious possessions,
they would have been our personal keepsakes, the photographs and the address books and little gifts from family
and friends. Don Hamman, a pastor-at-large for O.M. who
had flown in to be with the crew immediately after the
accident, understood this. Our possessions had been forcibly taken from us, he explained. Now it was time to
give them of our own free will, as an offering to God.

Don asked us to write a list of the things we most regretted losing. Then, after dropping our lists into a container one by one, we went outside. As Don set fire to our scraps of paper we put our arms around each other and sang: 'The cross before us, the world behind us . . . No turning back, no turning back'. More than a few of us wept during that little ceremony, but we also experienced a feeling of release – and a new resolve. Whatever we decided to do after we parted from each other, there would be no turning back from our service to God.

Around the world another reaction to the shipwreck was already gathering momentum. It came from the very young and the very old, the rich and the poor, from almost every country the *Logos* had ever visited. The message came spontaneously, and it was always the same: 'You must replace the *Logos* and go on. There must be a *Logos II*.'

In the United States, children were the first to present O.M. with a jarful of savings totalling $11.87. Gifts – often representing a sacrifice – also started pouring into the British office. Christians in Brazil managed to raise $10,000. Some contributed rings, necklaces, even a freezer.

A twenty-seven-year-old disabled woman sent a cheque, explaining, 'Tears came to my eyes at the loss of this beloved ship. $10 is a large sum for me but I really want to help'.

'I grew up in Taiwan as a missionary kid and I can remember visiting your ship anchored in Kaoksuing,' wrote another person. 'Even though I was too young to fully understand the ministry of the *Logos*, I was impressed with the uniqueness of it and the importance of it. May this small gift help you continue your ministry.'

Messages full of encouragement arrived from the young people aboard the Youth With A Mission ship, *Anastastis*. From another vessel, a US Navy chaplain addressed a letter:

From the saints of the *USS San Jose*, to the saints who sail the seas for the Lord . . . We know the trials of the sea and how dangerous the peril can be. Our hearts rejoice over the protecting hand of our Lord on the men, women and children of the *Logos* when she was broken on the rocks. We pray that this offering may be used to further the work of Christ Jesus through you.

During the five months following the shipwreck I worked at the US mission headquarters in Atlanta, investing all my efforts in publicity for the 'Launch *Logos II*' initiative. By the summer of 1988 the fundraising was well under way and the search had begun for a new vessel. It was time for me to move on.

Operation Mobilisation was just setting up an International Communications department in London and I knew that it needed a writer. The job would mean producing news releases, brochures, slide shows and other media for the whole O.M. world. Since to this point all of my experience had been confined to the ships, this seemed like a good way to expand my horizons. I agreed to move to England in the autumn.

Meanwhile, in July, I had an assignment to cover an international reunion of O.M. alumni in Holland called 'In Touch'. This gathering was actually the first such event in the mission's twenty-five-year existence, offering a rare opportunity to talk face to face with some of the 'old-timers'. Many of these rugged individualists had since gone into other movements or pioneered their own, such as Frontiers and People International.

By the end of July my old sidekick Susie Burton and I had completed the official 'In Touch' photographic report. Susie was returning home to New Zealand; I still had a month before the start of my new job.

The summer months are considered by most missions as prime time for short-term, student-oriented outreaches.

Operation Mobilisation recruits traditionally get their feet wet on summer teams. These campaigns are now called 'Love Europe': one to four weeks of fast-forward, cross-cultural evangelism all over the Continent that generally inoculate participants against an ordinary life for ever. After hearing some of the hair-raising escapades of campaigners I felt in no way deprived at having missed out on this particular piece of action. A number of leaders, however, insisted that August was the ideal month for me to get acquainted with Eastern Europe.

When an Australian friend of mine told me she was leading a team to Hungary I took the path of least resistance. I agreed to string along with Doreen and observe. Perhaps I could pick up a good story or two, as Eastern Europe, still under Communist rule, was wrapped in mystery for most of the West. My friend did tell me to bring my sleeping bag along, but it never seriously sank in, until too late, that this was to be a three-week *camping* expedition.

Maybe you remember the old song, 'A Tent or a Cottage, Why Should I Care?' Anyone who asks a question like that has to be joking. Any normal, civilised human being can reel off a dozen sound reasons for preferring a solid roof to canvas.

Psychoanalysts would no doubt tell you my antipathy to camping dates back to my childhood. The Great Outdoors was at that time my family's only affordable option for getting away from it all. I suppose those trips could be called successful because we were always so glad to get *back* to it all again.

Our family's greatest talent was in picking camp sites that veterans of the outdoors wouldn't have touched with a ten-foot tent peg. When we came across an unprotected site on the top of a cliff, for instance, we couldn't think of a single reason why we shouldn't claim the glorious view. We learned the hard way when a gale swooped down on us and very nearly blew us into the sea, saturating all our belongings in the process.

Another exciting memory was the time we pitched our tent on the shore of an island. Unfortunately, this turned out not to be the lee side but the weather side, and we forgot to take the elementary precaution of checking the high-tide level. We woke in the middle of the night to the slosh of waves gently lapping into our home away from home.

And there was the wonderful night we abandoned our tents and fled to the car with swarms of bloodthirsty mosquitos in hot pursuit. We entertained ourselves all through the long, miserable hours before dawn by plotting our revenge on the sadist who had recommended this site. Shortly after that episode we sold the tent. No one offered any objections. And now here I was, nearly twenty years older and wiser, blithely committing myself to a suicidal camping mission behind the Iron Curtain.

All teams were directed to rendezvous for preliminary orientation at an Austrian camp ground just beyond Vienna. My friend Doreen and I arrived in the evening after a ten-hour drive. After a determined struggle we managed to erect our assigned tent and crawl in. Fortunately it didn't collapse until the next day.

As I lay on the hard ground with my face smeared with mosquito repellent, I reminded myself that some people actually paid good money for doing this. I punched my jacket into a pillow and spent the next few hours trying to find a comfortable position. Campers drifted by, talking and laughing. I ground my teeth. A peacock, apparently the camp ground mascot, strutted around the tents and contributed an occasional unearthly scream. Finally things settled down and I dropped off to sleep.

Loud voices just outside the tent woke me. I stirred, reaching groggily for my watch. It was 3 a.m. My aching bones felt like they were cast in concrete. Something told me I should visit the WC, but the idea of emerging from my sleeping bag, my only protection against the man-eating swarms, was unthinkable. I put off the moment until delay was no longer possible. Then in one frantic motion I unzipped my bag, unfastened the tent, and – clutching my little penlight – vaulted into the pre-dawn darkness. My neck was almost immediately broken as I fell over a tent peg. Clouds of mosquitos descended greedily for the kill.

At last I made it to the designated shack. No lock on the cubicle door, no toilet paper. By the time I dealt with this dilemma and stumbled once more across the tented obstacle course, I was fully awake. I lay glassy-eyed, scratching my bites, until our team was roused to help with breakfast preparations.

After a day of orientation which convinced me that I would never see my mother again, eighty of us began moving out in teams to Czechoslovakia, Yugoslavia, Hungary and Poland. Our vans would be crossing the borders at different checkpoints to avoid drawing attention. It was comforting to remember that O.M. had twenty years' experience of working in this part of the world.

My own team was made up of five women and two men, with two more East German men due to join us at our destination. Our van was crammed to the roof with camping equipment and personal gear, plus literature and donated clothing to give away. The unseasonable cold of previous weeks had been replaced overnight by a heatwave. Murphy's Law strikes again, I thought. I had packed all the wrong clothes.

A few hours later we rolled over the border and stopped. *Hungary!* The countryside was surprisingly pleasant, green and quiet and not at all what my overactive imagination had expected. We handed over our passports and photos for the visas they would hopefully issue us here, laughing and trying hard to act like ordinary tourists. Inwardly I was rehearsing all the things we were not supposed to say in case we were grilled.

Suddenly I froze as two policemen carrying rifles burst from the guardhouse and charged past us into the peaceful-looking woods. Minutes later a truck roared up, discharging a dozen more armed soldiers. A border alarm had been tripped by someone trying to escape the country. I watched in horror, willing the image in front of me to go away. But this wasn't TV; it was reality.

Another guard strolled over to check our van. I was sweating in earnest now, remembering all the Christian books, Bibles and tracts we had each stashed between layers of clothing. The official walked to the rear of the van. Doreen unlocked it, flirting a little and jokingly warning him in German to beware of the avalanche when she opened the hatch. He hesitated, then laughed and stepped backwards. 'Never mind,' he told her with a wave of dismissal. 'You can go.'

I nearly hugged him.

Our destination was Lake Balaton, a popular holiday spot not only for Hungarians but Czechs and East Germans. The first camp ground on our list was full to capacity, so reluctantly we drove to our second choice. We had prior information that this site was located near a swamp with a record-breaking mosquito population, so I had been fatally certain from the start that this was where we would end up.

Sure enough, the camp site was crowded but the manager magnanimously permitted us to squeeze our three tents into a barren patch meant for one that no one else wanted. The next day the expected two East Germans, plus an unexpected Nigerian companion, arrived. None of them had any camping equipment. The following week a Christian Czech family also wedged their tent on to our site. We were grateful for their help in translating, but things were a trifle too cozy for comfort.

The main idea behind camping teams was friendship evangelism. The German speakers (and that was everyone in the group but myself and Jan, an English girl) had no trouble at all making friends. Every day we had more and more campers dropping in for coffee or a meal. While the others chatted, deep into soul-searching issues, Jan and I busily flipped pancakes, cut up vegetables for soup, and washed never-ending stacks of dishes.

After a week of cooking on a two-ring portable cooker for

ten to twenty people, with no shade from the blazing sun and temperatures hitting 110 degrees Fahrenheit, my servant attitude abruptly cracked. I announced to everyone within hearing that I'd had it. I was fed up with sticky heat and ice-cold showers and dirty dishes; fed up with sifting ants out of the sugar every morning; fed up with looking like a measles case from mosquito bites. But this was not the worst part, I grimly assured my team members. The greatest frustration of all was not being able to *communicate* with anyone. After coming all these miles I hadn't found a single individual who could carry on a simple conversation in English!

My emotional outburst should have made me feel better, but it didn't. Most of my team-mates were younger than I was. They had looked up to me, and now I'd botched it. They stared at me with round-eyed astonishment.

Fortunately, they were an exceptional bunch. Now that they were aware that they had a psychotic in their midst, they made a careful effort to translate for both Jan and me. In the afternoons, when we alternated camp site children's programmes with open airs at the nearby beach, I began participating in mime and giving sketchboard messages. I even mastered a whole children's song in German that I can still repeat with great enthusiasm to this day, without understanding a word of it.

Hungary was even at that time enjoying more freedom than many Eastern Bloc countries and we had no trouble with the authorities. Still, Christian literature could be distributed only with discretion. Those who chose the way of Christ knew they would find careers blocked and educational opportunities limited. Such a decision was not made lightly – and those who made it had our respect.

Open airs at the beach did prove a challenge, but not for the reasons we had feared. East Europeans in general have a less than inhibited attitude about their bodies. Although ours wasn't a nudist beach (there was one of those nearby), it was disconcerting to find topless ladies in our audience. We concentrated hard on eye contact.

The sizzling heatwave continued almost to the end of our stay and finally broke in a violent electrical storm. I lay shuddering in my tent, preparing to meet my Maker.

Although everyone survived the night, the next day's downpour brought it forcibly home that the only thing worse than camping in the broiling sun is camping in the driving rain. As the deluge continued into the second day our intrepid leader, Doreen, broke down and consented to calling it quits. Our frugal living had left us with a small balance in funds. We blew it all that final night on a decent meal, hot baths and soft beds under the roof of a guest house. I suspect that our behaviour was a betrayal of true blood-and-guts missionary form, but that night was pure heaven.

Since that summer in Eastern Europe the walls have all come tumbling down. O.M. is able to send unprecedented numbers of young people to live and work in formerly closed places such as Albania, Romania, Bulgaria and Siberia. For those who would like to count themselves pioneers, the adventures are far from over.

13

The end of the rainbow

Is not God upon the ocean
Just the same as on the land?
James Thomas Fields
In a Strange Land

Like many Americans I had always taken an enormous interest in England and all things English. As soon as I began to work I saved enough money to visit Britain twice, and even wrote my first book about England's tragic Lady Jane Grey. But when I moved to London to join the International Co-ordinating Team in September 1988, I soon learned that visiting a place and living in it are altogether different kettles of fish!

Take, for instance, the matter of vocabulary. Contrary to popular belief American and English people do not speak the same language. I was informed that I was no longer wearing a sweater but a jumper, not opening a can but a tin, not eating cookies but biscuits. It was a long while before someone enlightened me to the fact that boot sales were not good deals on footwear. Even my spellings of ordinary words were no longer acceptable.

Adding to my cultural disorientation were such frustrations as buying appliances. Why did no one tell me that I also had to buy plugs for everything – *and* wire them on myself? In church I made myself conspicuous by launching loudly into the wrong tunes for hymns I thought I knew. When I was invited to tea the first time I ate a full meal in advance. Tea, after all, was only something to drink, wasn't it?

But the English were kind to this transplanted Yankee and living ashore definitely had its advantages. The International Co-ordinating Team (ICT), headed by George Verwer, was the ideal place to learn about O.M.'s work around the world. I was often able to glean the latest news from O.M.ers who passed through Britain on their way to or from their fields. As for the great city of London itself, I never tired of exploring its museums and art galleries, palaces, parks and multitude of other places of interest.

I did not have the English Christmas I was looking forward to that year, however. Two weeks before the holidays I flew to Gibraltar for a very special assignment.

As my plane circled above the angular Rock and dropped smoothly on to the dual-purpose highway/runway at its base, I was remembering the first time I'd come to Gibraltar, two years before. On that occasion I had sailed into port aboard the *M.V. Doulos*. This time I was coming by air to join another ship: the vessel chosen to replace the shipwrecked *Logos*.

Friend and former shipmate Em Namuco was waiting to drive me the short distance to the shipyard. I sat forward expectantly as we went through the gates, passing a gigantic container vessel and a Moroccan Navy frigate. And then Em was pointing at another ship and I saw the name freshly painted on her hull: the *Logos II*.

'I can't believe it, Em!' I laughed with astonishment. 'She's so big! She's beautiful!'

I should have known what to expect, of course, for I'd written the news releases after the bid for the ship's purchase was accepted in September. I knew this twenty-year-old, Spanish-built ferry was a third larger than the old *Logos*. But the 4,900 ton reality looming in front of me was awesome.

I hurried up the gangway and stepped through the yawning entrance to the car deck. This vast and oily space, Em enlightened me, would one day contain the staff dining room, clinic and training classrooms. I stood for a moment bemused, trying to picture it, then Em hustled me up to the mess on the next deck where most of the crew were still eating lunch.

'Attention, everybody!' he called. 'Let's welcome the first single woman crew member on *Logos II!*'

Good-natured clapping and cheering broke out and I grinned. Although my assignment was to record the events of the *Logos II*'s maiden voyage, I was officially signed on as stewardess: dishwasher, floor swabber, and cabin cleaner! Four married women were also among the twenty-eight other crew members who would sail from Gibraltar to Amsterdam where the ship would undergo extensive renovation; together we represented sixteen nations. I was pleased to recognise many old shipmates, some of whom had taken short holiday leaves from other jobs in order to serve as engineers and deckmen for this historic voyage.

After lunch I left my bags in an empty cabin and trailed Em on a bow-to-stern tour, peering into one after another of the deserted and derelict cabins. My first excitement soon faded to dismay.

The ship had formerly sailed as a passenger/car ferry between Spain and North Africa. The space available was clearly more than enough to accommodate a crew of 175–200. But the two-berth cabins were at the moment no more than closet size: adequate for a ferry but certainly not for long-term living. Walls would have to be removed to double the area of each cabin and drawers, shelves and closets added. Ceilings and bulkheads (walls) also needed complete refinishing. A number of cabins were to be redesigned as offices, print shop and classrooms for the school-age children aboard.

A large space in the forward part of the ship, lined with windows and formerly used as a dining room, was already alive with workmen. This area would be transformed for conferences, with a seating capacity of about four hundred. A second, smaller programme room aft was to replace the present movie theatre. The biggest structural challenge, however, was the plan to extend two afterdecks to create a large book exhibition area and public coffee bar.

By the time I finished the tour I felt dizzy at the thought of all the money, materials, and manpower that would be required before launching the ship into service. And yet – hadn't the 'impossible' already been achieved? This £1.15 million vessel had been purchased within a year of the ship-wreck through the sacrificial gifts of thousands of students, small children, old age pensioners, and church mission groups around the world. Surely God would provide the rest of what was needed.

The *Logos II* was scheduled to leave Gibraltar on 14 December. Soon after I arrived we learned that a radio officer would not be available until at least 16 December. A further complication was that the engine's air compressor, just reinstalled after repair, was still malfunctioning and would have to go back to the shop. Our departure was postponed to 16 December.

No one seemed surprised by the delay. The ship had been plagued by problems ever since her official pur-chase in Greece. On one occasion both of *Logos II*'s anchor chains tangled with the anchors of adjacent ships so badly that a diver and floating crane were needed to free them. That same night, a sudden violent wind caused the anchor to drag. Engineers got the main engine started just in time to prevent collision with another ship.

During the voyage to Gibraltar, a small fire broke out in the main engine room, filling the area with smoke. A few days later the ship met with a Force Eight storm. The violent rolling caused the flooding of the food store and refrigerator and blocked the bilge pipes. The next day, when the winds died, the engine decided to quit. When restarted it became so overheated because of sludge choking the fuel lines, it had to be shut down again. The *Logos II* was towed ignominiously into Gibraltar.

Soon after the ship berthed one of the generators blew up, flying metal narrowly missing the engineer on duty. The next week the air compressor broke down. To add insult to injury the volunteer cook turned up drunk and had to be dismissed.

Fortunately the whole of the *Logos II*'s maiden voyage was insured, so a portion of the major expenses would be covered. But some people, even among those on board, were beginning to voice doubts. Was this really the right ship? Might not all these problems indicate that Operation Mobilisation had somehow made a terrible mistake?

The engineers got their air compressor back on Friday and worked non-stop to reinstall and test it. The radio officer arrived, and by 10 p.m. on 16 December we were finally ready to cast off.

It was a perfect night. As we slipped silently out into the Strait of Gibraltar I stood at the rail, awed by the dazzling necklace of lights along the Spanish coast. Competing for attention on the other side were the lights ringing the Rock. And above them all, outshining their splendour, stretched a canopy of stars.

This was my first night at sea since the shipwreck. Although I was not normally a nervous sailor, I lay rigid and sleepless on my bunk through the long hours of that night, every unfamiliar lurch filling me with alarm. My pallor at breakfast the next morning did not go unnoticed. Captain Tom Dyer had been Chief Officer of the old *Logos*. He grinned at me understandingly.

'Trouble sleeping last night, huh? Don't worry – you'll get over it.'

He was right, of course, and it was a good thing because I needed every ounce of energy for round-the-clock duties in the galley and mess. Engineers who came straight from the engine room, leaving a trail of grease wherever they walked, were the bane of my existence. But one visit to their workplace silenced my complaints. Men who put up with those countless hours of noise, fumes and claustrophobia, I decided, deserved all of my sympathy.

Not to put too fine a point on it, the whole ship was a mess. Empty cabins were ankle-deep in cigarette butts, garbage and graffiti. Only a few of the toilets were usable and these had to be flushed with buckets of water.

115

The December cold penetrated everywhere: the only heat was in the galley. Wires dangled and rubble littered sections already being torn down for reconstruction. We were isolated in a bleak floating world, without very much of the season's cheer. Determined to do what we could, we women hung a few Christmas decorations and left cards and chocolate on everyone's cabin doors. During mealtimes we played carols in the mess. The men teased us, but we knew they were pleased at our efforts.

On the first Sunday I got up while it was still dark to set the tables for breakfast. The tables had no frames to keep the dishes from sliding off, so with worsening weather we resorted to using dampened bedsheets as tablecloths, setting plates and cutlery on at the last moment. After the last big storm the tables themselves had been nailed into place.

At 10 a.m., while the off-duty crew met in the mess for a short time of worship, the lights suddenly went out. Generators and engine came to a full stop. We waited tensely for sound and lights to return and someone reported that generator number three had been ordered shut down because of the strange noise it was making. We were now relying solely on number two, which was running unevenly. We could not possibly proceed into the stormy Bay of Biscay under such conditions. If generator number three could not be repaired during the next few hours, the ship would have to go into port.

The next morning the *Logos II* dropped anchor in the harbour of Vigo, Spain. It was a black moment. The captain called all of us together again to discuss the options.

Work on the generators might easily take as long as a week. Some of the crew were already overdue in other places, others were anxious to rejoin their families for Christmas. Even if repairs could be made more quickly, the captain pointed out, there was a chance the harbour in Amsterdam would close for the holidays and we would be left cooling our heels outside.

Tom made it clear that anyone with pressing obligations should feel free to disembark in Vigo. The ship could remain at anchor until after Christmas, if necessary, and complete the voyage with a replacement crew.

British Chief Engineer John Seaman spoke up. His biggest concern, he stated flatly, was safety. He did not want already overtired engineers making mistakes in their anxiety to complete the trip. Nor did he want any more freak accidents.

My blood ran cold as he described an incident from the previous day, when a fuel line suddenly sprang a leak and sprayed highly combustible liquid on to red-hot exhaust pipes. If a quick-thinking Swiss engineer had not managed to stop the leak with his hands until help arrived, the ship might have gone up in flames.

In the discussion that followed it became clear the majority of crew members wanted to press on: finish the repairs as quickly as possible and sail to Amsterdam. No one wanted to leave before the job was done. Looking at the begrimed and weary faces of the men around me, I understood their frustration and dismay. Why one more crisis on top of everything else? Why was the ship continuing to suffer these largely unrelated problems, most of them issuing from its heart – the engine room?

At the captain's suggestion the crew committed the next minutes to prayer. With one heart we confessed our bewilderment and our complete dependence on God. We also asked for his protection and deliverance. A few hours later those who were free prayed again, this time in the engine room.

Indian First Engineer Elon Alva observed that in the next hours the engineers worked together with a unity and spirit he'd never seen before. 'I couldn't hold them back! They were working eighteen and twenty hours each, and they accomplished in a day and a half what took a week in Gibraltar.'

To the amazement of everyone, the *Logos II* was once more under way by 6 p.m. on 20 December. We had lost only two of the crew, Mats and Roberta Johansson, who needed to return to Sweden. Spirits were high. We entered the notorious Bay of Biscay the next day, where another surprise was awaiting us.

'I have crossed the Bay thirty times,' Elon Alva told me, shaking his head, 'but I've never seen it like this! It's like a lake!'

Our Norwegian First Mate recalled the storms he had weathered during twenty years at sea. 'You see it calm like this sometimes in the summer, but never in winter.'

The *Logos II* sped across the Bay with the wind and tide at her back. On my way to the galley in the afternoon I paused at the rail, my attention caught by the arch of a rainbow. Even as I watched, the spectrum of colours faded and then reappeared in a different place – and then another, just ahead of us. I was suddenly reminded of that other rainbow that had arched over the old *Logos* a year ago, and the assurance: *Those who put their trust in me will not be disappointed.*

God had been true to his promise.

The *Logos II* put the Bay of Biscay behind her and romped into the busy English Channel traffic far ahead of the estimated schedule. On the morning before Christmas we heaved in sight of the Amsterdam breakwater and waited for our pilot.

The seas were rough, so rough that several other vessels in the North Sea that December morning were in distress. The pilot boat was not keen to deliver the officer qualified to guide us through the locks. But Pilot Ed Verbeek was not just any pilot. Ed had once served as Chief Officer of the old *Logos* for three years, and he was determined to be the man to guide the replacement ship safely to her berth.

Dutch friends and family members of the crew were waiting faithfully at the first lock, cheering us in. A Dutch Christian television team boarded to record the remaining few miles . . . and at last the *Logos II* came to rest in the shipyard that was to be her home for the next sixteen months.

The ship was still only a skeleton of what she would one day become, through an army of volunteers. But that first

Christmas on *Logos II* was probably as memorable, in its own way, as my last Christmas on the *Logos* just before the shipwreck.

I had come full circle during that incredible year — or perhaps it was only a half-circle, to the end of the rainbow.

14

The spice of life

'Can you always tell when a stranger is a friend?'
'Yes.'
'Then you are an Oriental.'
                    E. M. Forster, *A Passage to India*

My alarm clock detonated at 5 a.m., blasting me relentlessly
from my warm cocoon into the cold English dawn. During
the few months following my voyage to Holland on the
Logos II I had begun to settle into life as a Londoner. It
was now the Ides of March, 1989: take-off day for a six-week,
fifteen-thousand-mile journey to the subcontinent.

I scrambled into borrowed Pakistani tunic and trousers
and half an hour later a friend and I were dodging London
traffic, on the way to Heathrow Airport. The act of leaving
my jacket behind with him seemed symbolic – a sort of
shedding of all things familiar.

My assignment this time would take me first to the
extreme north of India, where 300 young men and women
were crossing the finish line of a rugged five-month O.M.
campaign called RUN '88, or 'Reaching Unreached Neighbours'. Since this was also Operation Mobilisation's Silver
Jubilee, celebrating twenty-five years of evangelism in India,
Gorakhpur would provide the perfect place and time to
interview leaders and collect some up-to-date stories. From
India I would head to Pakistan.

By the time I landed in Delhi the Ides of March were over.

It was one o'clock in the morning of a new world. After a long delay clearing customs I took a taxi to O.M.'s Hospitality House. Except for an occasional dog or street sweeper, the streets were deserted. It was odd to see India at such a low ebb, its great tidal flow of humanity temporarily dammed to a trickle.

At the house I was given a sleepy welcome and shown to the door of the girls' quarters. The room was pitch black but after some groping I discovered four beds and three bodies, dead to the world. I unpacked only what was necessary and undressed. My watch struck the floor, meeting an untimely end. I collapsed on to the unoccupied mattress on the floor.

Sleep, however, eluded me. I was overtired and the tropical night held too much strangeness. All too soon the others in the house started to rise and dress, babies cried, smells of breakfast invaded. I dozed off and on until someone thoughtfully brought a cup of tea. After a lunch of rice and *dahl* – a sort of runny bean mixture – I set out for the city.

The deserted streets of early morning were now awash with life. Colour, noise and smells bombarded the senses. I exchanged pounds for rupees inside the posh Imperial Hotel, a throwback to days of Raj elegance, then wandered happily through the street stalls. Carvings and bangles, earrings and ankle bracelets, toe rings and necklaces, sandals and rich embroidery of every conceivable hue and design lured the eye, competing for attention at bargain prices. Temptation nearly overcame me. I sternly reminded myself of the long miles ahead and confined myself to the purchase of an inexpensive watch, which, alas, promptly stopped ticking as soon as I got back to the base. Perhaps Mother India was trying to tell me something.

In any case, I made it on time to catch the overnight train to Lucknow that evening. Lucknow was O.M.'s training and mechanic base, where subcontinent vehicles were serviced and reconditioned. Since the city was on the way to Gorakhpur, I thought it was worth checking out.

I shared my third class women's compartment with four

other ladies plus their assorted offspring. After a night sprawled protectively over my luggage and struggling not to be thrown from the top tier of three sleeping shelves, kept awake by the constant wail of babies and hawking of *chai* sellers, I did not step on to the platform in Lucknow feeling altogether refreshed.

Fortunately a fellow O.M.er materialised and hired a bicycle rickshaw to take me to the base. I agonised the whole short distance for the scrawny young man who was pedalling the bicycle; probably I would have felt much better running alongside. It seemed like just retribution when one of my bags toppled off the back. I happened to look around just in time to see another rickshaw run over it. So much for my tape recorder!

All of my senses, however, continued busily to record the panorama surrounding me: skin-and-bones cart horses struggling under impossible loads, 'sacred' cows with the right of way wherever they pleased, the odour of spices permeating the air, glorious bright clouds of red and pink bougainvillea splashing colour against stark, whitewashed walls.

After a day at the Lucknow base, interviewing and taking pictures, I joined a group of friends from the base who were taking the overnight train to Gorakhpur. Their cheerful companionship did much to shorten the journey. By the time we reached the Bible Fellowship Centre the next morning, my fatigue was overcome by anticipation.

My previous acquaintance with India during the *Doulos* visit a few years before had given me a healthy respect for the quality of Christians in that country. In Gorakhpur, as I began to uncover the stories of individual O.M.ers, my respect deepened even more.

Harihar was one of the many young people who had come from a Hindu background. His father, retired from government service, was introduced to Christ through the witness of a friend and shortly afterwards most of the family had followed his lead:

I remember my father came to see me once when I was studying for my degree. He asked, strangely, what I would do if he died. I was not yet a Christian and he was concerned about me spiritually. One day after that he was attacked and killed for his faith by men in our village.

I became a Christian, but that same year my older brother became mentally ill. The money I had for my examinations had to go for his treatment. I dropped out of school and tutored children in order to support the family. The neighbours refused to help because we had broken caste. For a time they would not even talk to us. But later they accepted me and even sent for me to pray when someone was sick. Now another family has converted to Christ!

Harihar had refused to let his experiences embitter him. Convinced that God wanted to use him to reach out to others, the shy, slender young man joined Operation Mobilisation in 1986. Since then he had learned to speak English, Hindi and Bengali – and memorised two thousand verses of the Bible. 'How much you learn depends on how much you want to learn,' he stated simply.

Indira, a lovely girl aged twenty-one, also had violent memories to overcome. When she was three she saw her father murder her mother. He then turned the knife on Indira herself, cutting her leg deeply before her brother intervened. After Indira's release from a hospital, missionaries took the little girl to be raised in a Christian hostel, which she now regarded as home.

Indira was eager to tell me about her adventures from the recent RUN campaign. The opportunity that meant most to her, she said, was having a long talk with a Hindu girl her own age and leading her to the Lord. The girl died unexpectedly only a week later.

The city of Gorakhpur, which lies only a few miles from the Nepali border, has the reputation for being the mosquito capital of the world. In the past months an encephalitis epidemic had claimed hundreds of lives in the area. Although the danger had now receded the mosquitos hadn't, and we engaged in combat with these fiendish flying beasties every evening. They invariably drew more blood than we did.

Sweet release came only when we crept under our mosquito nets. I loved to lie there smugly watching the monsters vainly trying to get at me. My pleasure ended abruptly, however, when I spotted several holes in the net. I devoted my free time after that to mending the thing, but the holes wickedly continued to multiply.

The conference schedule suggested rising for personal devotions at 5.30 a.m. I considered this idea suicidal and refused to emerge from the safety of my net before 6.30. Even then the vampires were lying in wait, as the windows of our whitewashed hut had no screens or glass.

Monkeys paraded along the roof as well and the outside door tended to swing open. One night as we slept a mangy dog wandered inside and made himself at home. The poor creature seemed to take a shine to us, because he managed to sneak in a number of times after that, crawling out in the morning from under one of our beds. He looked so pathetic I didn't have the heart to drive him off, though neither of my room-mates felt the same compunction.

No matter how early I woke, my room-mate Esther was up before me, usually kneeling on the hard floor by her cot. Once or twice I found her crying and eventually she confided her distress that she would probably have to leave the mission. Her father was no longer able to work and she needed to help support their large family.

'But I want so much to continue using my life in God's service, full time!' she added. 'I don't know what to do.'

Esther and I kept up a correspondence after we parted and I was glad when she reported that her family's circumstances had improved enough to allow her to extend her service with O.M. The next year a marriage was arranged with a fine young evangelist and the pair began working together among an unreached tribe in the north-east. Esther was one of the lucky ones. Many young girls as well as men found it very difficult to find a marriage partner within their tribe or caste once they became Christians. Some eventually yielded to the enormous pressure of their families to marry Hindus.

For several days a hot wind blew over the camp ground, coating everything with gritty dust and tearing our carefully hand-washed clothes off the line. Several large tents also blew down. During a teaching session on Indian Church History the centre pole of the tent we were sitting in collapsed with dramatically perfect timing. Our instructor had just finished quoting from Isaiah 54:2, 'Enlarge the place of thy tent . . . spare not, lengthen thy cords and strengthen thy stakes!' (KJV).

The electrical power, always unreliable, disappeared entirely on the afternoon I was scheduled to hold a writing seminar for O.M. leaders. A generator was found to power the overhead projector, however, and everything proceeded on schedule.

Easter Sunday was a day of celebration. Men and women alike were astir before five, the girls excitedly washing and dressing in their best saris, the men looking slim and neat in *dhotis* or Western shirts and trousers.

My Indian sisters eagerly insisted that I wear one of their saris. As Esther draped me in soft, sea-coloured folds I marvelled again at the ways in which modesty is defined by different cultures. Who would suppose that in a country where it is indecent to show one's legs, it is perfectly acceptable to bare one's midriff? The proper wrapping of a sari is an art and so is the graceful wearing of one. I never really felt secure without half a dozen safety pins to hold it together. All the same, I had to admit the final result looked – and felt – exquisitely feminine.

My room-mates and I had been assigned the honour of acting out the biblical drama of the three women who visited Christ's empty tomb. I'm afraid our efforts inspired more hilarity than reverence. My sisters, bless them, were not natural acting types, being far too inhibited to do more than giggle or whisper, and I overdid my efforts to compensate. But no matter: even the laughter seemed like a natural part of the day.

Few travellers in India escape the curse of 'Delhi belly', and neither did I. Although I had to skip Easter dinner the discomfort eased enough by afternoon to allow me to watch my first cricket match. Oddly enough, I had never had the opportunity to attend a game in England, and I found following the rules harder than I imagined. I kept wanting to compare the sport to baseball, which doesn't work at all. But the hilarious running commentary throughout the match proved a great enough entertainment.

After filing two weeks' worth of stories, it was time to move on to Pakistan. Canadian field leader Dave Lundy happened to be travelling back through Delhi at the same time, so we shared the luxury of air-conditioned second class – a world apart, I discovered, from third! The increased space and security allowed me to sleep well during the fourteen-hour journey. To our surprise, a fellow traveller in the carriage identified himself as a former O.M.er, a converted Hindu who was now translating Bible study books into Hindi.

The passing scenery of Uttar Pradesh offered glimpses of prosperous, cultivated fields and small villages, each built around miniature Hindu temples. Here was living at its most basic. Nothing was wasted. We even saw cow dung that would be used as fuel, drying in cakes on the walls of many homes.

Reaching Delhi I was dismayed to find that Phil and Sheila Davies, the couple who ran the Hospitality House, were not at home; nor did anyone know when to expect their return. I needed to leave for the airport almost at once in order to catch my plane to Pakistan – and Phil had my air ticket! Not knowing what to do, I simply committed the problem to the Person in charge. At exactly that moment it dawned on Phil and Sheila as they were shopping that they'd forgotten about me. They rushed back to the house and bundled me and my ticket into a taxi, just in the nick of time.

Speeding to the Indira Ghandi International Airport, I took a few last mental photographs of India: my Sikh taxi driver, dignified in white turban and moustache, spoiling the effect by spitting out of the window; a mother dreaming on a doorstep with her naked baby, lost in their own private world; a cow marooned on a traffic island, placidly chewing its cud in the midst of blaring horns; fumes, dust, sweat, the merciless glare of the sun; sari-clad women perched side-saddle on the backs of motorcycles; and flowers – everywhere – in bright defiance of omnipresent poverty.

Ah, Mother India, you were right! In this timeless land, who needs a watch?

15

No place for a woman

No longer friendless in the world around us,
no longer helpless, no longer weak . . . It is only
your fancy that we sleep, yet unconscious.

Habib Jalib, poem written
for Women's Action Forum
of Pakistan

I fastened my seat belt for the Delhi to Lahore flight and
settled back to think about my next assignment. Benazir
Bhutto's surprise election as the first female leader of a
traditionally Islamic nation had captured the world's interest.
One of my goals was to find out if her government was
making a difference to Pakistan, not only to women but
to the religious scene at large.

I had to admit that I was nervous. This was my first visit
to this country, my first total immersion in a Muslim world.
Solo travel in India had proven remarkably easy. A stranger
with dark colouring and local dress can blend neatly into the
surroundings, so long as she keeps her mouth shut! Pakistan,
however, was an unknown quantity. The Salman Rushdie
affair had not put writers on top of the popularity polls and
I had no desire to excite attention.

When friends failed to meet my plane in Lahore I stifled my
first impulse to panic and exchanged some money to make a
phone call. A taxi driver approached. 'Taxi?' I shook my head,
but he trailed me hopefully to the telephone.

My friend at the other end apologised. Someone had actually met my flight, he explained, but failed to spot any Western-looking lady passengers. He instructed me to sit tight. I sat, feeling the taxi driver's eyes on me, not quite abandoning hope.

Men and women passed wearing the loose, elegant national dress called the *shalwar quamis* that I myself was wearing. I felt quite gratified that I had been mistaken for a national. Perhaps there wasn't anything to worry about after all. But that was where I was wrong. The problem was not that I was a Westerner, nor even that I was a journalist. My handicap was being a woman.

Travel writer Geoffrey Moorhouse has noted in his book, *To The Frontier*, that 'the only unpleasant thing certainly awaiting the stranger to Lahore is its traffic'. Lahore's traffic is most assuredly the stuff of nightmares. But any self-respecting, even moderately liberated female from the West will take issue with Moorhouse. My own first plunge into an Islamic society was an icewater shock from which I have never really recovered.

Like most people I knew that Pakistan, 'land of the pure', was carved from Hindu-dominated India to provide an independent state for Muslims. I had been prepared to see Islam woven into the texture of daily life. But what I could not possibly have grasped, until I experienced it myself, was the quality of life that Islam assigns to half its population.

For hundreds of years, devout Muslim women have been kept in place by the system of *purdah*. Purdah literally means 'curtain', and implies social separation and concealment – a form of sexual apartheid. Those who keep purdah emerge from their homes only when necessary, and preferably in the company of their husband or older brother. In public they wear a modestly draped head scarf or, better still, a head-to-toe concealing *burqa*.

The Pakistani *burqa* is most often two pieces of black polyester: a long-sleeved, ankle-length robe, and a scarf which covers the hair and ties under the chin. The scarf has two additional veils, one or both of which may be dropped over the whole face according to the level of security desired.

The outfit is worn over ordinary clothing and, in temperatures that soar to 120 degrees Fahrenheit, black is not the coolest choice. An additional safety hazard exists when the veils obscure the vision. I have tried on the Afghan version of the *burqa* and it is even worse: one solid tent of cotton falling from the crown of the head to the feet, with only a screen of netting over the eyes to allow navigation.

I have to admit, however, that the *burqa* is a practical form of self-defence in Pakistan, for women who venture out alone on the streets are considered fair game for all forms of unwanted attention. During my first walk through Lahore I was treated to stares, touching, suggestive comments and kissing noises. Within a few days I found myself conforming to the defensive behaviour of other women, scuttling as fast as possible from one point to another with my head covered and eyes downcast. By keeping 'eye purdah' – avoiding eye contact – and moving in a random path one might escape the hands of passers-by. But it left me feeling vulnerable, degraded – and outraged.

I was told the public harassment of women is called 'Eve-teasing'. It is actually an arrestable offence and husbands who accompany offended wives are expected to exact punishment on the spot. The woman who has no such defender may remove her sandal and bash it over her offender's head. Of course, nine times out of ten, he has already made his getaway into the crowd.

Sexual considerations aside, getting around in the city of Lahore is not for the faint of heart. Ox carts and donkey carts and small horse wagons that carry passengers, called *tongas*; three-wheeled auto-rickshaws, bicycles, motorcycles and buses all clog the road with equal determination to jostle each other aside for the right of way. I even saw a few camels being pressed into service. Not surprisingly, accidents are commonplace.

For those who enjoy the thrill of sustained terror I can

recommend the 'Flying Coach'. (A friend, by the way, once saw one of these lettered 'Fleeing Couch'.) This express mini-van service connects most of Pakistan's major towns and cities. Drivers are undoubtedly selected on the basis of how reluctantly they apply the brake pedal. I remember sweating profusely all two and a half hours to Faisalabad, and not just because the air-conditioner was broken. The worst moment was when I caught sight of a legless man painfully pulling himself across the narrow road just ahead of us. I closed my eyes, so I can never explain how we missed hitting him.

On the return trip that night I was the only lady passenger and therefore awarded the front seat beside the driver. This allowed me a ringside view of a hundred near-collisions. The driver seemed to derive his greatest glee from the old game of chicken, seeing how close he could come to an oncoming vehicle before one yielded to the other. I had to be scraped from the floor upon arrival.

In spite of the fact that they are usually overcrowded and hot, the bazaars of Lahore are an Aladdin's cave of delights. A cheerful attitude of 'You make it, we'll fake it' generally prevails, offering shoppers a wide range of cheap imitations of trademark products – everything from luggage to shampoo. Best of all are the sections devoted to clothing and accessories. Fabulous bolts of vivid silks and satins, cottons and polyesters, drape the aisles enticingly, with vendors sitting cross-legged, tape measures at the ready around their necks.

For the customer in a hurry, ready-made 'Punjabi suits' are available; more commonly, however, a lady selects material for a tailor to sew to her exact specifications within a day or two. I settled for two practical cotton outfits off the rack which I still use for casual wear. In my opinion they are the perfect synthesis of beauty and comfort.

Lahore is an ancient city. Near the top of every tourist's list must be the Lahore Fort, created and added to by successive moguls. Shah Jahan, of Taj Mahal fame, built the Shish Mahal – Palace of Mirrors – within the fort as a home for his empress. The thousands of tiny mirrors covering the walls are arranged in lovely mosaic patterns. These and the lace-like marble screens over the windows of the women's area give one an idea of the splendour of the Shah's empire.

A number of interesting mosques are open to the public. I visited the Badshahi Mosque, one of the largest and oldest places of worship in the world, with an estimated capacity of 100,000 people. After removing my shoes as required I ran across the red-hot pavement of the vast central courtyard with bare feet, yelping in pain. When the attendant chased after me I thought he was going to rebuke me for my unholy haste; he only wanted, however, to ensure that I covered my head.

The mosque's marble floors and rich carvings, the spacious vaulted arches, were indeed worth seeing. To anyone accustomed to standard church buildings with pews and platforms, it is always a surprise to find such simplicity within Islam's houses of worship. There are few furnishings at all, really, besides prayer mats. But probably the star attraction of Badshahi Mosque is the display of relics of Mohammed: a walking stick, a lock of hair, slippers, and even – quite the most startling of all – his underwear!

Mosques are conveniently located on every street corner, so the five times daily call to prayer is a sound you don't escape. The loud wail of the evening prayers, rising in unison from thousands of voices all over the city, never failed to send a shiver through me. It was like the lament of lost souls.

My visit coincided with Ramadan, the Muslim holy month of fasting. All but the most necessary work is suspended during the hours of fast, in order to preserve energy. At the specified moment of sunset everyone falls ravenously upon food and drink and the feasting continues through the night. Ironically, it is estimated that more food is consumed during the month of fast than any other month! But most restaurants are closed during Ramadan. When friends took me to a hotel for lunch, we were required to sign a statement declaring that we were either (a) non-Muslim, (b) travelling, or (c) sick.

To learn about life 'behind the curtain' I accompanied a mission worker on visits to a number of Muslim women in their homes. Without doubt, these ladies are among the warmest and most generous of hostesses I have encountered in any country. A social call by someone outside their own extended family was a novelty for most of them, especially a visitor from the West. Women and children of the household invariably crowded around. A cup of tea or coffee would be pressed upon me – or a child might even be hurriedly despatched to the neighbourhood shop to buy a cold Coke or sweets for their guest. Then the questions would begin. Where was I from? Why was I visiting Pakistan? How did I like it? And of course the inevitable and all-important question: was I married?

The ladies were, of course, consistently astonished that I was not. Marriage is almost universal in Muslim cultures, where a man may take up to four brides. A girl is often wed by the age of sixteen or seventeen and her happiness after that depends a great deal on her ability to produce children – preferably sons.

Hanging over every family with daughters is the burden of getting them married. As in India, dowry payments demanded by prospective in-laws can be astronomical and many a bride's family has gone deeply into debt to meet them. One sweet-tempered girl I know has had to accept the fact that she will probably never be wed. Her family cannot afford the dowry that would be required for a girl with a bad limp, the legacy of a childhood illness.

The options for women are slowly expanding, however. One female educator told me that more women are fighting for their rights, for more education and jobs outside the home. But there are complex issues involved. One of these is class distinction. She gave the example of her sweeper's daughter: 'Farah is ten and should be in school. But a school would mean expenses her family can't afford. Even if the fees were somehow paid and she were educated, what then? She would no longer be content marrying an uneducated man. Yet no one in a higher class would marry Farah because she would still, after all, be the daughter of a sweeper.'

I particularly recall the visit to a young woman who was

born and brought up in England. When Nabila came of age, her family arranged a marriage for her in Pakistan. I asked her if the adjustment had been difficult. She smiled, her expression holding both bitterness and resignation. 'You live in England,' she responded finally. 'You know what it is like. What do you think?'

Matters of dress and appearance are of great importance in a world of limited horizons. In one household a young woman knelt before my chair and slipped several bangles over my wrist. She had noticed that I had none and correcting the lack of adornment was both a gift and necessary courtesy. The same day, as I took my leave of another family, a girl shyly fastened a necklace around my throat, exactly matching the colour of my dress.

Such open-handedness impressed me. I had to learn never to admire a picture or other object, as my hostess might immediately make a present of it. And even during Ramadan everyone insisted that as a foreigner I should accept refreshment. I felt most uncomfortable eating or drinking in front of my lady friends and would gladly have abstained, but they would not hear of it.

The women I met were intensely curious about the world in which I moved so freely. Whenever conversation moved to my personal faith, they listened to that as well. Several gladly accepted the books we carried, and one even purchased an inexpensive *Injil* – Urdu New Testament. But I began to understand the implications of a Muslim woman trying to follow Jesus Christ. The repercussions would be instant and extreme.

One lady I was told of who professed faith, the wife of a journalist, was forbidden any further Christian contact. Her Bible was confiscated and she was watched continually by the other wives, threatened with the loss of her children. How could anyone's faith survive such pressure? Whether or not hers did, I never found out.

The Church of Pakistan owns a surprising number of imposing stone buildings, but only a very slim margin of the population are called Christians. And, unfortunately, the majority of these are only nominal Christians, by default of not being born Muslims or Hindus.

But there are genuine followers of Christ in this land. I met with some of them in the heart of Lahore, in a church in the truest sense of the word: no actual building, only a small circle of men and women in a courtyard. Most of them were blind.

In a 'survival of the fittest' society the handicapped do not generally fare very well. There is no time or money in Pakistan to waste on those who make no useful contribution. And yet, as I watched the faces of the men and women around me that day, I knew these people were not to be pitied. They seemed unaware of the burning afternoon sun, the thousands of flies that caked every surface, the abject poverty surrounding them. Their voices rose in uninhibited praise to God even as a mullah's call to prayer rang out from a nearby mosque.

These forgotten ones who had once 'sat in darkness' had seen a great Light. It seemed to me that they had the advantage.

16

To the frontier

For the North
Guns always – quietly – but always guns.
Rudyard Kipling, *One Viceroy*
Resigns: Lord Dufferin to
Lord Landsdowne, 1888

The Russians withdrew from Afghanistan in the spring of 1989. As far as the world was concerned, the nine-year war was over. While I was still in Lahore I went to see an exhibition of photographs in the American Centre which bore the euphoric title, 'Afghanistan: A Nation Goes Home'. A week later I was confronted by a far harsher reality.

Peshawar, 'Frontier Town', lies to the extreme north of Pakistan, just thirty-five miles east of the Afghanistan border. It is the first major settlement one reaches after the Khyber Pass. When I saw it, the city had swollen into a miniature Afghanistan, refuge for hundreds of thousands who had lost everything but hope.

I had travelled north on the invitation of a relief agency called SERVE. SERVE was just one of about seventy organisations in Peshawar set up to assist Afghan refugees, but it was rather unique. It was – and still is – supported by world Christians who want to demonstrate God's love tangibly to suffering people. Its other distinction is its personalised, multifaceted approach to relief work. The letters of SERVE stand for Serving Emergency Relief and Vocational

Enterprises, and its programme is designed to meet both immediate and long-term needs. This includes the provision of emergency aid, an Eye Hospital, blind rehabilitation, solar oven production and distribution, reforestation, public health, and a vocational carpet weaving project.

The first night my SERVE friends gave me a crash course on what and what not to do in polite Afghan society. 'Don't shake hands, pass food or eat with the left hand. Bread is considered holy so don't put it on the ground or lay it upside down or feed it to the dogs. Never blow your nose in public. Do not point the soles of your feet towards anyone; feet are unclean. Remember that an invitation has to be issued three times before it will be accepted.' All of this convinced me that I was sure to commit some unforgivable *faux pas* and set off another war.

After the Lahore exhibition I expected to see refugees stampeding back to Afghanistan. What I found were freshly opened 'tent cities', sheltering more than forty thousand men, women and children who had fled to Pakistan *after* the Russian withdrawal. The face of the enemy had, perhaps, changed, but the war raged on. Afghanistan's Freedom Fighters – *mujahideen* – had sworn to resist the Najibullah government to their last breath.

The war had now reached its second generation. Little boys carried to safety at the start of the Soviet occupation were now teenagers, old enough to join – or replace – their brothers or fathers in the *mujahideen*. Untrained, inexperienced, the survival odds of these new recruits were marginal. It was a rare refugee family that had not paid its dues in blood several times over.

The morning I went to interview a SERVE doctor's wife, I had to push through a crowd of widows and children crouched in front of the gates of the doctor's house. They reached out to touch my hands, my face, imploring me in a language I did not understand, but with a desperation all too clear. The doctor's wife told me that sometimes the men going by threw stones at the women, berating them for exposing themselves to the public's gaze. Still, they came. They had no man, no husband or brother, no choice. They wanted only to survive.

Camouflaged ambulances continuously arrived from the front, shuttling the wounded to Peshawar's overflowing hospitals. The small staff of SERVE's Eye Hospital treated over twenty thousand patients a year. About one-third of the patients were victims of mines or bombs. My heart turned over as I looked into the scarred and ravaged faces – so many of them children.

SERVE began an orientation and mobility service for the blind when it realised no one else was helping them. The Malaysian staff member who handled the women's side explained that after field workers located blind individuals in the camps, they took them to the Eye Hospital for examination.

'Sometimes they can be cured!' she added enthusiastically. 'Just last week we took four children to the hospital. Doctors discovered that all four could have cataract operations and regain their sight!'

Staff worked with blind refugees in the camps until they gained enough confidence to move around on their own. Eventually they learned to do basic household tasks and often progressed to contributing to their family's support.

I still remember my first client. Bibi Wala had scarcely left her tent in six years. She was in her fifties, dirty and cold. I never saw a face so miserable and dejected.

The transformation in her now is marvellous. She is still old and thin, but she has a smile on her face and even laughs and jokes with us! Because she can move freely by herself she has a place in the community, a sense of worth.

For Ross, a New Zealand sheep-farmer turned forester, there was a different kind of satisfaction. His job was to supervise the growth of thousands of trees that would provide Afghans with shade, fuel and animal fodder. With an eye to the future, he was also assisting with a reforestation project inside Afghanistan.

Ruth from the United States was introducing solar ovens, made by Afghan employees, into the camps. Afghans traditionally depended on wood for cooking, but wood was scarce. Sunny Pakistan was the ideal spot to harness solar power for cooking. Most of SERVE's own staff lunches were cooked by the sun.

The agency's Public Health branch wrote and distributed practical information on safety and hygiene. Their latest booklet for children focused on mine awareness, one of the greatest hazards that Afghans face in resettlement. By conservative estimates, between ten and twenty million unexploded devices needed to be cleared. Some were disguised as toys, pens or watches. When cannisters containing 'butterfly mines' were dropped from planes, each one had in turn launched thousands more plastic deathtraps into the surrounding landscape. There they could lie in wait for weeks, months, years.

The doctor's wife asked if I planned to go over the border. A Japanese journalist had gone into Afghanistan the previous month, she told me. After filing her story the woman had stopped just short of the Pakistan border for one last photograph. She took one step backwards – and got blown to pieces. I decided I didn't need to go over the border.

Staying in the home of SERVE Directors Gordon and Grace Magney provided its own thrills. One day a scorpion scuttled through the front door, the next day a bullet paid a visit through the front window. Grace was unmoved; she had a whole collection of them, she said. Guns and gunrunning were part of life on the frontier. We passed through one nearby village which boasted that it could duplicate any firearm in existence. The whole length of Darra's main street was lined with stalls showcasing pistols, rifles, and machine guns.

Drug-trafficking was also big business. I noticed small foil packets of hashish openly displayed in some bazaars. The bright fields of poppies in tribal areas were known to yield a rich harvest in opium, despite the Pakistan government's attempts at control.

Peshawar was a political powder keg, overpopulated by desperate Afghans with their *mujahideen*-backed interim government, Pakistanis who resented the Afghans' growing numbers, and Communist provocateurs intent on fanning discontent between the two.

Seven months after I met him, SERVE's tall, personable office manager, John Tarzwell, disappeared without a trace. John had been due to leave Pakistan within a few days to join his wife Leeanne in Canada for the birth of their third child. Although most believe responsibility lies with one of the extremist factions, there was no ransom demand and authorities failed to turn up evidence. In the summer of 1991 the case was closed. Perhaps we will never know the truth.

The war in Afghanistan has now been over for some time. Though *mujahideen* factions continue to fight among themselves, the refugees have been told they can go home.

But what is left for them to go home to? The Russians' scorched earth policy reduced the fertility of the country's agricultural soil by 35 per cent. Transportation routes linking cities have been obliterated, irrigation systems, springs and wells deliberately filled in. The levelling of forests has created a long-term shortage of building materials. And many of the 'brains' of Afghan society, the professionals and intellectuals who weren't killed, have long since scattered to begin lives in other countries.

SERVE continues to give as much aid as possible, although it struggles with shrinking support. Many other relief agencies have folded. The world has tired of sustaining the Afghan effort and has turned its attention to other areas of need. So what happens to them now, these men, women and children who have quietly packed up their few belongings and disappeared into the decimated remains of what used to be their country? Nobody seems to know. And nobody seems to want to know.

17

Curtain going up

May shipwreck and collision, fog and fire,
rock, shoal and other evils of the sea be
kept from you; and the heart's desire of those
who speed your launching come to be.
John Masefield, *Launching of the Queen Mary,*
The Times, 25 September 1934

The refurbished *Logos II* was launched on 24 April 1990.
When she sailed to London I was on the quayside with
dozens of others to wave her in with balloons and banners,
half blinded with tears and cheering myself hoarse. At last,
almost twenty-eight months after the death of the old *Logos*,
her replacement was ready for commissioning.

The timing couldn't have been more perfect. A tidal wave
of change was sweeping over Eastern Europe, and during the
months of June, July and August the *Logos II* would have a
chance to ride the crest. When I was offered the position of
press officer for her maiden voyage, I didn't hesitate.

At the end of May I joined the ship in Bremen, West
Germany, laden with luggage, laptop computer, and the
double pushchair the captain's wife had inadvertently left
behind in London. Fortunately this last item didn't need to
fit into my cabin. The space assigned to me was down
in the belly of the ship in the single women's section, a
cupboard wedged between the chain locker and communal
toilet/shower. The cabin contained only a narrow bunk and

clothes cabinet. Humble, but all my own! The chief steward assured me that the carpenter – after finishing work in the book exhibition and other priorities – was planning to add shelves and a fold-down desk top. Alas, I knew better than to assume that day would dawn anytime soon.

The *Logos II* was scheduled to call at seven Baltic ports in East Germany, Denmark, Poland, Finland and the USSR, as it then was. The contrast between Bremen, in the West, and Rostock, our first stop in the East, hit us forcibly as soon as we went ashore. We felt as though we had stepped fifty years backwards into history. The shops were quaint and old-fashioned, offering limited choices. Cans and jars on grocery shelves looked home-made. Yogurt and Coke had only recently made their debut and, although expensive, were proving wildly popular.

East German cars were all curiously alike, differing only in colour. The chief virtue of the little Trabant was that it was cheap. The car was basically made of compressed paper and it could run for decades without rusting. One man assured us he was on the waiting list for eleven years before becoming the proud owner of his own used model.

Rostock greeted the *Logos II*'s floating bookshop with wonder. Thanks to donations by Swiss and German Christians, we were able to sell forty tons of German books at nominal cost. Happy shoppers carried away armloads at a time, exclaiming, 'We could never buy such books here before!' A number of buyers were self-declared atheists, frankly searching for answers. Books that didn't sell by the end of our visit were unloaded for distribution among the churches in East Germany.

It was startling to meet men, women and children who knew little or nothing about the Bible or Christianity. School children asked the basics, like 'How old is God?' and 'Where does he live?' Some of the adults we talked to weren't aware of the meaning of Christmas or Easter, or that the New Testament is part of the Bible.

The number of Christians was small, but God's church had

survived. Part of the way through one programme on board, a man in the audience began to sob. He walked to the front and embraced the speaker. As he tried later to explain, never before had he heard such things spoken of with such liberty in his country. His tears were tears of joy.

They possessed so little, and yet local believers insisted on providing the crew with fresh daily supplies of bread, milk, and eggs. The day before we left an elderly lady turned up with a paper bag full of coins. She had been saving them for years to supplement her retirement, she told us; but now she felt she should give the money to the ship instead. Our protests were firmly ignored. Her offering amounted to $173.

Several Russian cruise liners berthed directly astern of us in Rostock. One evening the crew of one ship invited our men for a few games on their funnel deck. Our crew were delighted to accept, and even though the Russian players made short work of us in volleyball, we managed to hold our own in basketball and even managed to win. Good-natured camaraderie prevailed and before leaving we were happy to present forty Russian New Testaments and tracts which the men seemed equally eager to receive.

Some hours earlier I had shown the lady purser around the *Logos II*. She spoke perfect English and was clearly amazed both by the family atmosphere and the low cost of books in the exhibition. 'In Leningrad people will rush to this ship!' she predicted. 'There will be long queues!' I fervently hoped we would have a chance to prove her right. Moscow had not yet given its sanction to our visit.

Discovering the existence of a Russian army base in Wismar, a dozen of us took a train to the city to see what we could do. We held a few open airs in the quaint town centre and then found the military camp. Although we weren't able to gain admittance, an officer allowed us to distribute tracts and books at the gates. The dozens of black-booted soldiers who passed in and out accepted the Testaments with great interest. Some men stopped to remove the pins from their uniform lapels and presented them to us as a gesture of thanks.

One army wife was particularly pleased. 'This is the book I have wanted to read, but I could never find one!' she exclaimed.

'We need more of these books in our country,' a senior officer said with conviction. When it was time to catch our train, he offered to ensure that the rest of the literature was distributed.

A number of us on the ship used our day off to visit East Berlin. It was a seven-hour round trip by train, but it was worth it to stand at the Brandenburg Gate, where freedom had so lately broken through. Even then we couldn't cross the checkpoint to West Berlin without re-entry visas. Awed, we peered over at the 'no man's land'. Piles of dirt indicated where mines had been dug up in preparation for making the place into a park. Russian street signs and statues of Lenin were still prominent, but unification was unstoppable. Already shops were demanding payment in Deutschmarks rather than Ostmarks. In Alexanderplatz, entrepreneurs blatantly black-marketed West German electronics. The fabric of Communism was unravelling before our eyes. East Germany would soon be history.

Sailing from Rostock to ultra-modern Copenhagen and then to Gdynia, Poland, was enough to knock anyone into culture shock. Take the cost of a simple ice cream cone: in East Germany we only spent the equivalent of fifteen cents for a serving: in Denmark the price skyrocketed to a prohibitive $1.50 to $2.00. Imagine our glee when we arrived in Poland and discovered we could buy an ice cream for ten cents! Of course, with Poland's exchange rate of 10,000 zlotys to a dollar, it meant carrying around wheelbarrows of local currency to pay for anything.

But Poland had a distinct old-world charm. I knew it from our opening day in port, when a gentleman caught my hand to his lips in a polite salute. I was badly shaken, but determined to carry off my part with *savoir-faire*. This sort of treatment, I decided, was the kind a woman could get used to very easily.

The Poles must have liked the *Logos II* as well, since we saw a record ninety-two thousand climb aboard during our two-week stay. Happily the visit coincided with the Baltic Sea Festival. Throngs of pedestrians were drawn to the waterfront to visit several ships, which, besides ours, included a graceful three-masted training frigate.

To be Polish generally implies being Catholic, but this did not prevent anyone from attending our programmes or buying books. The demand for Christian reading material in the Polish language, in fact, far exceeded availability. To encourage the nation to generate its own literature instead of depending solely on the West, the *Logos II* held a Writing Workshop. I was a bit disconcerted when a contingent of Hungarians also attended the workshop; translation into two languages reduced the time that we had together. But their enthusiasm made the effort worthwhile.

That Fourth of July in Poland brought another new experience. I had at first rejected the invitation of friends to go with them to a concentration camp several hours away. Films and photographs alone of the Holocaust devastated me – I didn't think I could face the reality. But after a lot of thought I changed my mind. It was something I had to experience: as a writer and as a human being.

It was good to get away from the ship. The Polish countryside was soft with green fields and flowers that were not very different from those at home. I was just beginning to relax and enjoy the outing when we arrived at our destination. Then I was lost, swallowed up by the barbed wire and watchtowers and the main gates of Stutthof: the Gates of Death.

'Once you enter these gates,' one hundred thousand prisoners had once been brutally informed, 'you are no longer a person, you are a number. And the only way you will leave is through a smokestack.'

We went into the building where the camp's new arrivals had been forced to exchange their clothing for a 'uniform'. Confronted with the mountain of shoes left behind by those men, women and children now long dead, I felt as though I'd been kicked in the stomach.

The exhibits in the barracks that were still standing were labelled in Polish. The guided tour was not in English, either, so I just wandered around the camp on my own. I don't believe I could have taken in any more. The gas chamber, the ovens, the abandoned wooden cattle cars, the ashes enclosed in a memorial, required no words, only tears.

'It is raining here in Stutthof,' I wrote in my notebook, trying to release some of the horror. 'It is right that the heavens should weep, should always weep in this place. Here no flowers should bloom, no green grass grow. Let the earth lie stricken, mute witness to the obscenities committed here, for ever.'

I shared the experience with my writing class the next day. They were quiet. Afterwards a woman remained behind to confide with some wonder that I was the first person she had ever heard admit to having Jewish blood. 'Jews in Poland don't identify themselves,' she explained matter-of-factly.

I was shaken by her revelation. Was it possible, all these years later, that there was still so much fear and distrust? Surely in such a place, surrounded by so many ghastly scars of hatred, history would never be repeated? But perhaps man's heart didn't change, I thought. Perhaps it was essentially the same in every age, in every country, until it was transformed by a force outside itself.

The musical drama *Les Misérables* happened to be playing in a music theatre near the ship while we were in Gdynia. Since seats were available for the equivalent of only $1.20, a group of us enjoyed an evening out. I had seen the musical performed in London, but in Poland – so newly experiencing freedom from Russia – the drama of the barricades took on a heightened significance. I found myself profoundly moved.

Les Misérables tells the story of a people's defiance against oppression. Pride, desperation and courage were

146

all factors behind their success. But more than anything else, I realised, the battle was won through the power of unselfish love.

Poland's hope – the hope for all who inhabit our earth – lay in acknowledging the source of that love. God himself.

18

The Russian revolution

*I have begun to sense what Russian writers have long
revealed: that this is a place where the human spirit
is made to struggle, thereby becoming fuller as well
as more repressed.*

George Feifer, *Moscow Farewell*

The impossible had taken place. All through the preceding
weeks in Eastern Europe, Moscow had stubbornly with-
held permission for the *Logos II* to visit Russia. The
ship's line-up personnel had almost despaired. Finally the
Deputy Mayor of Leningrad made a surprise move and
took matters into his own hands. 'I am not here to play
at perestroika,' he announced to immigration authorities.
'I'm here to *make* perestroika!' He invited the ship to
Leningrad.

On 26 July 1990, the *Logos II* sailed up the Neva River
with the hammer and sickle fluttering from her mast overhead.
Significantly, our berth was just downriver from the Winter
Palace where another ship, the *Aurora*, had fired the opening
shots of the 1917 Revolution. The *Logos II* was making history:
the first foreign vessel in seventy years to be open to the
public.

'You will like Leningrad. It is a beautiful city,' Finnish
friends had enthused in Helsinki. The first sight of its
imperial dignity did not disappoint me. The city – now
renamed St Petersburg after its creator Peter the Great – is

rightly called the Venice of the North. Miles of canals wind between lavishly proportioned buildings, all reflecting a dignity and excellence that must have been dazzling in the days of the czars.

Major tourist attractions like the Hermitage museum are still carefully maintained. The gilt spires of the Admiralty and Peter-and-Paul Fortress and the dome of St Isaac's Cathedral also glitter grandly on the skyline.

But, looking more closely at the majority of Leningrad's buildings, the illusion of grandeur vanishes. I was appalled at the peeling and crumbling facades, broken windows, neglected roads: the sad testimony of a city whose glory has long since departed.

Leningrad distressed me and I tried to analyse why. Certainly the place was no more crowded or polluted than other cities with a population of five million. The buildings were shabby and fashions outmoded, true, and there was a pervading air of poverty that I hadn't expected. But certainly I'd seen far worse in Africa and India.

Perhaps what troubled me was the blankness upon the faces I passed; the outright rudeness as well, and not just by shop clerks but by the man on the street. More than once a pedestrian behind me simply shoved me out of his way. Even in the poorest slums of other countries, people had not lost their caring response to one another. They were still able to draw strength from a mutual faith. It was this dimension that was absent in Leningrad. For the first time I was seeing the result of a system that denied the soul. Was this really the sort of people Communism produced? The experience of one *Logos II* couple seemed to provide a chilling confirmation.

Em and Marilyn were browsing around a major department store on Nevsky Prospekt when a man just in front of them suddenly collapsed. As he fell he struck his head and began to bleed profusely. My friends immediately knelt beside the man to see what they could do. To their astonishment, no one else made a move to respond. No one even indicated concern. The cashier nearby kept totalling figures without a pause, sales clerks continued attending customers, and passers-by spared little more than a glance. Eventually my friends managed to staunch the man's spurting wound while another foreigner coming upon the scene telephoned for help.

During my short time in Leningrad I also heard of a number of cases of medical malpractice. I met two victims personally: one a young wife and mother, permanently crippled by inept back surgery and unable to work; the other a seventeen-year-old son of a Baptist minister. This boy had been born with normal intelligence, but administration of the wrong drug during an infant illness tragically left him severely retarded.

Russians spoke of such incidents matter-of-factly. When I asked why they happened, they shrugged. The doctors were poorly paid, they said, some just did not care about those they treated. Others were concerned, but lacked equipment and drugs.

In dramatic contrast to the 'man on the street' were those who had refused to conform to the system. For resisting their government's ultimatum to embrace atheism they had been hunted and persecuted. Yet many had managed to survive, and when we came to Leningrad they were the first to meet us, full of warmth and love. In spite of their suffering they were whole human beings. 'We've been waiting for you,' they told us with tears of joy, 'for a long, long time.'

In two weeks thirteen thousand Russian men, women and children visited the *Logos II*, full of awed curiosity. Unfortunately, Soviet law forbade us to sell books either on or off the ship. For the first time our book exhibition was purely an exhibition and we were keenly aware of the frustration this created.

'Why do you come here and show us books that we cannot buy?' everyone demanded. When I told *Izvystia* reporters about the ban, their newspapers carried an indignant article headlined: 'IT'S OK TO LOOK BUT NOT TO BUY!' Many people stood around reading the books for hours right in the exhibition. A steady number of titles, particularly Bibles and

New Testaments, disappeared from the shelves every day. The staff cheerfully replaced them. Eventually the ship was allowed to donate an additional 8,000 Bibles and 4,000 New Testaments to the churches for distribution.

The Russians' frenzied eagerness for Bibles jolted me, as I suppose it would any Westerner who has grown up spoiled by unlimited access. We learned that black market Bibles sold for 400 or 500 rubles – two to three months' hard wages. One delegation travelled a thousand miles from an eastern republic in the hope of obtaining copies. I was particularly touched by the sixty-five-year-old lady who spent twelve hours on trains to get to the ship. She had her own Bible, she declared proudly, unwrapping her treasure from several protective layers to show us. When we offered her another copy to take back to her friends, she burst into tears.

That first Saturday a few of us were invited to attend a local baptism. To reach the river where it was being held took an hour and a half via Metro, train, and on foot along a muddy path. The rain was coming down when we set out, but I was assured with smiles that the rain always stopped for the service. It did.

At the end of our trek wound a small and very cold, copper-coloured stream. For many years the Christians I was with had carried out their baptisms secretly, meeting by night in a forest and using only candlelight. Even now that they could gather openly, baptisms were not treated lightly. Some of the candidates had waited two years to prove the reality of their faith. One of the men now being allowed baptism was a former Communist Party member. The church had learned to take no chances.

What an honour to stand with that little group and sing from our hearts, 'How Great Thou Art'! As I sang in English and they in Russian, an older woman beside me slipped her arm around my waist. Her son had been one among the many sent to prison for his faith.

As solemn as the occasion was, I had to choke back my laughter when the nine baptismal candidates emerged from the bushes after changing clothes. All were wearing identical white lab coats, the women's hair tied severely back in white kerchiefs. They looked exactly like an open-air operating team. Fortunately I was able to hide my unseemly mirth behind my camera. One or two medics on the scene might not have been a bad idea, actually. The river was so icy, even in July, that one lady all but passed out. The pastor must have been made of very stern stuff indeed. I learned that baptisms were performed right through the autumn until the river froze over.

We were all ready, after distributing the customary flowers to participants, to adjourn to the church for further worship, prayer and tea. The church was actually the pastor's apartment, with the family's beds pushed against the wall of the combined dining room/bedroom. Only about half of the 150 members were able to squeeze in at a time. Repeated applications to the government to renovate another building for use as a church had, sadly, been refused. But the people were united in praying and fasting for a breakthrough. Since my visit I have heard they finally received the necessary permit.

It was depressing to see the many church buildings that had been confiscated by the government and turned into warehouses or museums. One Baptist church I attended had just been returned to the people after being used for decades as a factory. The outside was totally derelict, but the interior was freshly whitewashed, bright and clean and crowded wall to wall every Sunday with worshippers.

All of us on the *Logos II* had expected close restrictions on our activities. Instead we experienced almost unlimited freedom to distribute literature and conduct open-air programmes when and where we pleased. Probably the most unbelievable moment for me was singing a hymn in Russian on the steps of the Museum of Atheism and Religion, right in the heart of Leningrad. A friendly guide inside the museum even offered to pass out tracts along with the tour brochures!

On another satisfying day 130 crew members and local young people spread out over the city to give away 290,000 'Life' Scripture booklets. At my position near the entrance to a Metro station my supply was exhausted within a few hours. Russians were clearly startled to be offered anything free. Only a few responded with a belligerent '*Nyet*' or other words I was just as happy not to understand. Others tried to give us flowers or kopecks in payment. During all of our time in Leningrad I never saw a tract discarded. Some pedestrians, after reading a page or two, shyly returned to request a second copy for friends. A city councillor afterwards remarked to ship leaders, 'This is a very famous booklet! Everywhere you go on the Metro people are reading it!'

Those who read the literature often brought their questions to the churches whose addresses were stamped on the back. Others came to the ship. 'Who is Jesus?' they wanted to know. 'Why did he come?' 'Is it necessary for me to go to church to pray?' One man announced, 'I don't believe in God but I want my children to. Have you got more literature?'

The films we showed on board, even old classics like *Ben Hur* or *Quo Vadis*, drew people to stand in patient lines hours in advance. The movies themselves ran for four or five hours, but audiences were never in a hurry to leave. They lingered long afterwards to ask questions, talk with crew members or pray. Often when I passed the lounge I glanced in and saw men and women on their knees.

The city of Leningrad gave the red carpet treatment to the *Logos II*. Buses and guides were furnished for the crew to tour the fabulous Hermitage art museum. The Ministry of Culture even arranged a special concert by the string ensemble of Leningrad Conservatory's Symphony Orchestra. Everywhere we were reminded that this was the city of genius – the residence of Tchaikovsky, Nijinsky and many more of the finest artists and musicians of all time.

With only a little money in our pockets, we were gratified to discover that Western currency could stretch a very long way. Many taxi drivers and shop owners in fact refused payment in anything but dollars. It was a great temptation to trade money on the street, where vendors offered three times as many rubles as one could legally receive in a bank.

Beryozka shops, specialising in souvenirs for the tourist trade, dared the most outrageous exchange of all at fifty-six kopecks per dollar. My shipmates and I were, of course, too tightfisted to patronise such places, although it would have saved a lot of time. The buying procedure in most Russian shops was enough to shred the patience of Job himself.

The first challenge for the foreigner was to locate the right kind of shop. Few businesses had window displays and were only identified by small signs in Russian. Once inside you joined a long line of customers awaiting the attention of the clerk. When your turn arrived you pointed out the item, examined it and received a slip of paper stating the price. The article then went back to the shelf while you joined another line in front of the cashier's desk. When at last you had paid the designated amount, you had to return to the original counter line to await your turn once more, hand over the receipt to the clerk and obtain your purchase.

There is always, however, a certain satisfaction in beating the tourist system. On one memorable occasion a number of us were able to attend a live performance of the ballet classic, *Swan Lake*. During the intermission we overheard an American woman complain to her husband about the poor location of their seats.

'What can you expect for eleven bucks?' he snarled.

We couldn't repress a grin. Our party had secured its tickets from a street booth, as the Russians did. We had paid the equivalent of fifty cents for the best seats in the house!

Even this price, however, would be an extravagance to the average Russian who might earn only two hundred rubles or thirty-five dollars as a good month's wage. A doctor averaged about three hundred rubles. One neurosurgeon I met worked a second job as a journalist to make ends meet. Another doctor drove taxis. From what I observed, only the elderly *babushkas* were exempt from working, and they were expected to care for the children or stand in endless lines for food.

Getting around on the Metro, tram, or bus was the best deal in town: tickets cost less than a penny for any single distance. The Metro was a shining example to the world. Floors and walls were almost surgically devoid of litter, graffiti or any sort of advertising. An eagle-eyed guard stationed in a booth at the foot of every escalator (some of the longest in the world) ensured they stayed that way. When a shipmate brashly rolled a coin down the centre rail, a volley of Russian threat exploded through a loudspeaker. I thought we would be annihilated on the spot.

Russian Christians could not seem to show enough of their welcome. Each day they delighted in bringing little gifts of flowers, souvenirs, sweets, postcards. A young volunteer couple who had helped with translating and other work brought me a Tchaikovsky recording. And at the end of our visit the churches prepared a loving feast for the crew members, presenting the *Logos II* with a samovar and a large bag of sugar – one item in a long list rationed in Leningrad.

Because we hadn't been able to earn any money in the book exhibition we were concerned about paying the port fees. Would the authorities require rubles or hard currency? To our astonishment they wanted neither. They would be satisfied, they announced, with a gift of forty Bibles.

The vast scale of need in Leningrad gave us all a deep reluctance to leave. Knowing other believers were waiting for us in the Baltic states, however, we said emotional goodbyes to our many new friends and started for Estonia. As our vessel moved down the Neva River we noticed many of the crew members of nearby ships waving enthusiastically. One man stood at the highest elevation of his ship, took off his shirt and flourished it as long as we were in sight.

A few hours into our voyage the captain called for the customary lifeboat drill. For further practice, he ordered the boats actually lowered to the water with volunteer crew. We were just completing this exercise and climbing the rope ladders back on board (a much harder feat than it looks, by the way!), when a large Russian patrol boat roared up alongside, enveloping us all in noxious clouds of diesel fumes. The commanding officer demanded to know what we were doing. I would have thought that it was rather obvious, but the officer was not to be put off lightly. He requested and received permission to board and address our captain.

The *Logos II* crew and Navy crew, meanwhile, eyed each other with enormous interest. We debated whether we could offer the sailors Bibles or invite them to supper. Alas – we and our cameras were soon ordered to clear the decks.

It emerged that our lifeboat practice was in violation of Soviet water regulations. As it was apparent we had not been advised of this fact, we were allowed to proceed without further incident. We did so with all haste, chastened and very much sobered to realise how closely we were being watched.

Tallinn, Estonia, was a picturesque, medieval-looking city of 500,000 people. Just after tying up beside the Town Hall (formerly called the Lenin Palace of Sports and Culture) we were informed that the Estonian Supreme Soviet had two days before declared the legality of its own national flag. We rushed to replace the hammer and sickle on our mast with the appropriate pennant of blue, black and white! Although the republic would not declare its independence from the USSR for another year, nationalistic fervour was running high. To keep the peace, all of our programmes on board, including my Writers' Seminar, were conducted in both Russian and Estonian. A few of the public came from as far away as Uzbekistan to attend. Others used their precious petrol ration.

Thanks to the Estonian Ministry of Culture's determined efforts, we were allowed to sell books in Tallinn. The exhibition drew book-starved residents like a magnet. When Leningrad heard the news that books were available, a number of people actually took the nine-hour train journey south to buy them as well.

Popular authors and speakers Jill and Stuart Briscoe joined the *Logos II* in Tallinn. When it was time to leave, Stuart addressed over seven hundred Estonians who braved the bitter wind and rain to attend the quayside Farewell Rally. Standing small and insignificant among the crowd was my friend, Luule.

I had met Luule after serving as MC of a Sunday afternoon programme in the ship's lounge. Several of the audience had lingered to talk or ask questions, and I was anxious to move things along because there was another meeting scheduled to begin. Besides that, I was already overdue at a small party I'd been invited to attend. Such opportunities for relaxation and good food were rare, and I didn't intend to miss this one!

I had finally discharged my duties and was heading towards the exit when a volunteer intercepted me. Another lady was waiting to see me, he said and added as an afterthought, 'She doesn't believe in God'.

He led me to the woman and at first sight of her my heart sank. She was middle-aged, heavily made up, with a face I can only describe as hard. I had no inclination to debate the existence of God with this woman, but I forced a smile, shook her hand, and sat down.

Luule's bitter diatribe erupted at once – all in Estonian. As the volunteer translated her words into English I kept my eyes fixed on hers, wondering at the years of unhappiness that I read there. At last the flow of words slowed and died. I took her hand, trying to bridge the gulf between us.

'I understand that you have been ill-treated, and you have suffered a great deal,' I said slowly. 'But Luule, you are directing all your hurt and anger at the wrong person – the one who loves you most.

'I know that God can help you because he has helped me. But he won't force his way into anyone's life, Luule. Confess your need of him, ask his forgiveness for the wrongs in your own heart that sent Jesus to the Cross. Then he will begin to heal you, from the inside.

'I can't promise an instant solution to all your problems,' I finished. 'It doesn't work that way. But he'll help you face them. You won't be alone any more.'

Luule's face suddenly crumpled. It was as though an infected wound had been lanced and was being washed clean with her tears. I knew she was free at last to heal.

We embraced and prayed together, she in Estonian, I in

English. After that she came back several times to see me. I wondered that I had ever thought Luule's face hard, for now it was transformed by a childlike eagerness.

She came to the farewell rally, too, in spite of her frail health and the blustery winds. And when the ship began to move away from the quayside she waved as long as we were in sight, standing alone – but no longer lonely.

Luule and I have continued to correspond since that summer. She has reported slow but definite progress in her personal life, encouraged by the local church and Bible study. Most of her physical problems have disappeared. And she calls the day she came on board the best day of her life.

Our final port in what was then still called the Soviet Union was Riga, Latvia. Here again we found a republic in transition, with the sparks of independence already beginning to flare. Russian soldiers were still very much in evidence, but Riga's main avenue, formerly called Lenin Street, had just been renamed Freedom Street. And the floral tributes that used to be laid at the foot of Lenin's bronze statue now, in brave defiance, adorned the towering Liberty Monument.

'What is the difference between Latvia today and Latvia fourteen years ago?' A pastor visiting *Logos II*, just returned from a fourteen-year exile, smiled. 'First, freedom. Second, freedom. And the third difference – FREEDOM!'

Another pastor who led one of our teams to a high-security men's prison admitted that he had himself been interned in that prison for six years because of his faith. This was the first time visitors had ever received permission to go inside for a meeting. The crew members were more than pleased to be invited back a second time to hold a gospel concert for the men.

My women's prison team got the same enthusiastic reception, once we got past the commandant. This facility had been named after one of Lenin's KGB favourites and the interior was just as grim as the exterior, although we had been told it was one of the best. The only exception was the commandant's plush office, where we were given a very long wait while our passports were inspected. In spite of the man's politeness we found it very hard to relax. Perhaps it was the effect of Lenin's portrait glaring down at us from the wall.

At long last we were led away to the women, who had been assembled and waiting for I don't know how long in a huge, dreary meeting room. To our chagrin they got to their feet to stand at attention as we came down the aisle. We did our best to loosen up the regimented atmosphere with music and mime and personal introductions. Then with the help of a Russian translator I shared a few thoughts from Psalm 130.

'Out of the depths I cry to you.' Looking up from the first verse into the sea of faces in front of me, I could only guess the depths of the misery each had gone through. Would the Psalmist's words mean anything to them, I wondered? Could these women identify with David's anguish, and understand that Jesus's atonement was for them as much as David?

Miraculously, I saw that they did understand. With the dawning recognition of God's love, faces softened. The eyes of a few women filled with tears.

It was time for the noon meal to be served. Unexpectedly, the warden announced that any women who wished to stay could do so. Forty or fifty of them crowded to the front. We talked and prayed with each one, putting our arms around them and weeping with them. When we finally left we gave out Scripture portions in Latvian and Russian.

'Is it possible to visit the children?' we asked the warden as she conducted us out. We knew at least twenty children belonging to the women inmates were housed in separate quarters. But permission was refused. Later we learned that visitors were rarely allowed access to the children because of their more or less permanently unwashed, ill-clothed, and malnourished condition. Prison food was in fact so deficient in essential nutrients that both women and children were frequently ill and the only doctor for the prison had little equipment or medicines. He was also, reputedly, drunk most of the time.

Riga's officials showed the extent of their appreciation for the *Logos II* visit by waiving all fees for berth, tugs, and agent. As an added concession we were permitted to purchase a hundred tons of fuel oil at inexpensive local prices.

On departure day twenty customs and immigration officers scoured the ship for three hours before issuing an 'all clear'. In spite of their efforts, we discovered a stowaway in the forecastle two hours out of port. We had been warned of the serious repercussions for harbouring a Soviet citizen. The *Logos II* had no option but to turn around and head back.

A pilot boat met us part of the way to take the young man off. As he disembarked, weeping, we could not restrain our own tears. The Iron Curtain had lifted enough for a Christian ship to slip through for an incredible summer. But there was still a long way to go.

On 3 September I celebrated my birthday at sea and logged the following in an exultant letter home: 'I have just spent an hour at the helm of the *Logos II*! The captain and first officer were both on the bridge keeping a careful eye on me, but before long I had the hang of it. What a thrill to feel that great ship respond to the wheel. The captain said he suspected I'd done a few hundred miles off the Maine coast!'

I was immensely proud of myself, and it was the best possible finale to my three months on board. A few days later, after a hair-raising passage around John O'Groats, we sailed up the Firth of Clyde to Glasgow. It was, for me, the end of the voyage.

19

The Orient, express!

The city . . . appears at the foot of its
radiant mountains: it blazes like a
great flower of light with neon stamens
and petals of floodlit stone.

James Kirkup, *Streets of Asia*

'Sorry, but I'm afraid there are no more seats available in Non-Smoking.'

The harassed-looking assistant at the airline reservation counter in Amsterdam turned away and I gave myself a mental kick on that June morning of 1991. Why hadn't I reserved in advance? A dozen hours of inhaling tobacco fumes and I would land in Hong Kong with a head fit only for an ash tray.

Once on board I made a last, desperate appeal to the stewardess. She checked the forward section of the plane and reported one empty seat. In a flash I was down the aisle, climbing between two passengers who had probably been congratulating themselves on the extra space.

The pleasant-looking Asian man on my right seemed distinctly familiar. I had noticed him before in the terminal building, and wondered if I'd seen him before at some O.M. conference. I contemplated trying the old cliché, 'Excuse me, haven't we met some place before?' but promptly discarded the idea. Obviously the man didn't recognise me, or he would have said something.

After takeoff we exchanged polite conversation. Was I going all the way to Hong Kong, he inquired? Business trip or holiday? I obligingly launched into a detailed rundown about my job with Operation Mobilisation and the summer outreach I was covering called 'Love Hong Kong', rounding it all off with a few carefully chosen words about my personal faith. My seat-mate listened with flattering attention.

'And what about you?' I finally wound up. 'What takes you to Hong Kong?'

He hesitated a moment longer, then burst into irrepressible laughter. 'The same reason as you,' he admitted. 'I'm going to Love Hong Kong, too!'

Daniel Chae, as he proceeded to reveal to my chagrin, had been invited as one of the principal instructors at the week-long training camp preceding Love Hong Kong. He was a veteran O.M.er, an experienced leader of Love Taiwan campaigns, and was presently living with his wife and children in London while pursuing doctoral studies.

We were both struck by the fact that the only two passengers bound for Love Hong Kong in a plane of four hundred should end up as seat-mates. On the other hand, it seemed typical of our heavenly Father's consideration. The remaining hours in the air and in transit in Bangkok flew by far more pleasantly than either of us had anticipated.

The approach to Hong Kong International Airport is both exhilarating and heart-stopping. The airstrip is built as a causeway into the sea, making it seem like the wildest impossibility to thread a plane between so many skyscrapers and stop before ditching. But the pilot brought off the challenge with finesse and we were soon thankfully treading terra firma.

Like many people I had always imagined the 'pearl of the Orient' as an island. Hong Kong actually includes 235 islands besides the one most favoured by postcards. Add to them the Kowloon Peninsula and New Territories stretching up to the People's Republic border, and the land area totals over 409 square miles. That's not a lot of space for six million people. Housing is inclined to be very steep, both financially and architecturally. The surprise is that there are still so many unpeopled islands and restful green hills designated as parkland.

Since Love Hong Kong wasn't yet under way, it was arranged for me to stay a few days in the New Territories with a young nurse named Donna Chung, a former missionary to Pakistan. As Donna and I left the terminal building together the heat struck me like a physical blow. Late June and July was the typhoon season and probably the hottest time of year to visit Hong Kong.

We jumped on a bus, which immediately joined a long line of other vehicles held up by road construction – quite typical, Donna assured me, of this ever-expanding city. I was already sweating profusely when a downpour forced the closing of the bus windows. The heat intensified to sauna conditions, but I was diverted by a sign above our heads that sternly cautioned, among a long list of other things: 'DO NOT SPIT. BEWARE OF PICKPOCKETS', and 'DURING TYPHOONS ALL WINDOWS MUST REMAIN OPEN'!

Donna lived in a traditional walled village several hundred years old, peopled mostly by Chung relations. She and her brother were the only members of her family who had converted to Christianity. The two now shared a tiny flat, but continued to eat most of their meals with the family next door. Although everyone spoke Cantonese and conversation was somewhat awkward, I cherished the genuine slice of Chinese culture that most tourists never sample.

Chopsticks, I admit, did prove a problem. Not naturally dexterous, I had always avoided the use of these eating implements, and when, before the trip, I applied to a Malaysian friend for a lesson or two, she had poured scorn on the idea. Hong Kong was one of the most sophisticated world-class cities, she assured me: I would have no trouble at all finding forks.

Her words returned to mock me through all my subsequent

163

battles with the rice bowl. And it taught me a lesson. Western amenities such as knives and forks belong to the tourist ring of glass-and-steel shopping centres, hotels and Pizza Huts. Once you step outside these you find the heart of Hong Kong. And that is pure Chinese.

To my delight, I discovered that my old ship, the *M.V. Doulos*, was at anchor in Hong Kong harbour. The vessel had been scheduled to sail to the Philippines a week earlier, but a major eruption of Mount Pinatubo had delayed her departure. It felt strange and wonderful to step aboard the old girl again after more than four years. She didn't appear to have changed much. Only the faces of those who served as staff and crew were different.

Invited to stay the night, I lingered a long while against the rail, enjoying the unceasing spectacle of Hong Kong harbour traffic. The ferries and cargo ships and sampans that paraded by fit every category from tiny to titanic, ancient to modern.

Crew members described how, during their passage through the Taiwan Strait a few weeks back, they had thrown over a thousand plastic bags into the sea. Each one contained a Mandarin New Testament that would undoubtedly be picked up by the Chinese fishing boats nearby. It was gratifying to hear that the *Doulos*'s 'fishing' efforts were still going strong.

Little did any of us suspect, as we relaxed together on that warm June evening, the terrible events that lay only a few weeks ahead.

The tragedy was to strike in Zamboanga, the *Doulos*'s last port of call in the Philippines. During an international music programme held by the crew on shore, two men suddenly burst into the auditorium and lobbed grenades into the midst of performers assembled backstage. Karen Goldsworthy of New Zealand, aged nineteen, and Sofia Sigfridsson, eighteen, of Sweden were immediately killed in the explosion. Thirty-two other crew members were hospitalised with injuries ranging in severity from shrapnel wounds to broken bones. The reason for the attack was never made clear, nor were the perpetrators ever captured.

For the next few days I explored Hong Kong Island. Finding my way around the efficient and comfortably air-conditioned tram system proved easy. But the frantic tempo of life, the sounds, smells and sights of the Orient, soon glutted my senses. I was overwhelmed by this city with its throngs of pedestrians scurrying purposefully in every direction. I was staggered also by the great disparity between the wealthy and the poor. Surely it was only my imagination that most of the cars on the road were luxury models? But it is a fact: Hong Kong has more Mercedes Benz per square mile than any other country in the world.

I picked a clear day to ride the famous tram to Victoria Peak, which boasts the most stunning panorama of Hong Kong. The Star Ferry, shuttling every few minutes between Kowloon and Hong Kong Central, is another 'must', providing an exceptional view of the skyline for only a few cents.

But one of my favourite excursions was to Aberdeen, the city named a hundred years ago by a homesick Scot. The harbour is home for hundreds of sampans used by families year-round, and for a few dollars it is easy to hire a boat for a fascinating look around. Those who can afford to splurge might consider sampling the cuisine of one of Aberdeen's glamorous floating restaurants.

Not even the most casual visitor to Hong Kong, however, can remain oblivious to the fact that this shining jewel in Britain's crown is 'a borrowed place living on borrowed time'. 1997 reminders are plastered on every marketable product from T-shirts to posters. I even found a board game called 'Trial 1997'.

'Hong Kong,' declares the game's creator, the New Frontier Enterprise Company, 'has entered a transitional adventure without historical precedent where a full-fledged western-style capitalist society will be absorbed by a communist giant; a pledged one-country, two-system arrangement designed ultimately to harmonise all of China's lost territory. Can it work? Will it work?'

Tens of thousands of Hong Kong's citizens have decided

it won't and more professionals are joining the exodus every day. But it would be inaccurate to say that everyone who can afford to leave is choosing to do so. Developers like those behind the new Lantau Island airport and the giant shopping complexes rising close to China's border are anticipating a rosy financial future.

The issue of emigrating Christians is a sensitive one. Most of the believers I spoke with, both clergy and lay people, were slow to condemn. As one leader chose to explain, 'The Lord knows some pastors will be needed amongst immigrants in other countries. Only they can know the Lord's will in their decision.'

'The church wants to strengthen believers in the Nineties,' maintained another pastor, 'whether they are in Hong Kong or Canada.'

Late in June Donna Chung and I travelled up to Fanling, near the Chinese border, where Love Hong Kong participants had gathered for a week of preliminary training. The idea for this outreach came from Stella Chan, O.M. Hong Kong's leader and a lay minister of one of the colony's largest churches. With the shadow of 1997 growing ever darker, she felt the need to strengthen the church at grass roots level. The 140 young Asians taking part were largely sponsored by their home churches in Malaysia, Singapore, the Philippines, Taiwan, Australia, Korea and Hong Kong itself.

For most of these men and women this was their first brush with a culture outside their own: a different language, different foods, different ways of thinking. 'It's good to be the minority for a change!' observed Craig, one of the Australians. At the same time I sympathised with his struggles with noddles or gruel each morning at breakfast and rice every lunch and supper!

The training programme was concentrated and demanding. For me the greatest eye-opener was the seminar on Chinese culture and folk religion. Through Dr Agnes Liu of the China Graduate School of Theology, I began to appreciate the extent to which spirit worship dominated every aspect of this part of the world.

Following the lecture I ate lunch and then stopped in at the building where I was staying. Dr Liu was in the lounge, counselling one of the Hong Kong recruits and praying with him in Cantonese. As I was passing, to my astonished horror, I saw the young man begin to choke. His hands flew to his neck as though he were being strangled.

I had always wondered how I would react to an overt demonstration of evil. In that moment I felt outrage. How dared Satan? No one – no power in heaven or earth had the right to attack one of God's own! Other staff members gathered to claim Jesus's authority and healing. Within just a few moments the boy exclaimed again. But this time we saw gladness, not agony, lighting his face. He was free.

'Dr Liu's message was a turning point for me,' the young man explained to the rest of the Love Hong Kong participants some weeks later. 'I was very weak and ill when I was very small so my mother took me and dedicated me to a god. I always felt an inferiority complex after that. When I listened to the lecture I was very nervous. I shared this with the doctor and she and other staff prayed. I felt the evil power leave me, and now I can control myself. Now I have peace in my heart.'

The pervasive reminders of spirit worship in Hong Kong reminded me of Africa and India. We seldom walked into a home, shop or restaurant that did not contain a shrine to the gods. Many times on the street the smell of incense would draw my attention to a tin on the pavement containing smoking joss sticks. Red banners (red is considered the luckiest colour) with Chinese characters commonly adorned the doorways of many houses to ward off evil spirits. And diviners were consulted as a matter of course in all decisions, even those as petty as where to move furniture.

Shopping with a Chinese friend in Fanling market one day, we passed a stall stacked high with what appeared to be play money of all denominations. Curiously, I picked up a pile.

'Carmen, look at this!' I called my friend over. Along with the Cantonese inscriptions on one side was the English inscription, 'Bank of Hell'.

Carmen nodded. 'You will find money for sale in all the markets. See the pictures of the gods on each bill? This is burned for deceased relatives – so they can use it in hell.'

She pointed to colourful packages strung along the stall. 'Not only money is burned. You can buy clothing, miniature wristwatches or radios – even car models.'

Carmen went on to explain that for most Chinese, reverence for one's elders continues on after their death. The souls of the deceased must be assisted in their journey to heaven by carefully prescribed rituals.

'It is usually the eldest son's responsibility to perform such duties for deceased family members,' she added. 'That is why it is almost impossible for him ever to think of becoming a Christian. Family loyalty is strong.'

Our camp's proximity to the People's Republic proved too tantalising to resist. On a blazingly hot Saturday the Korean women's leader and I hopped a train to the border town of Wo Lu. Standing on the bridge that formed the no man's land between Hong Kong and China, we stared at the high fence and barbed wire lining one side of a dirty-looking river. We crossed to the other side of the bridge, but that was as far as we got. Americans were permitted through if they purchased a visa, but Mee Un, a South Korean, was not allowed that option. We turned back, disappointed.

At the end of the basic training week, teams moved out to link up with local churches in Kowloon, the New Territories, Hong Kong Central and Macao. I cast my lot with six teams that were based in Sha Tin, the fastest-growing city in the New Territories.

High Rock Christian Centre in Sha Tin was not exactly the Hong Kong Hilton. Encircled by high-rise apartments, the rustic hostel was perched on the top of a pinnacle that could only be reached by a steep and narrow footpath. Climbing this trail was tricky enough even without luggage. Encumbered with all of our assorted suitcases, literature boxes and other equipment, we were left in a state of near-collapse.

I did enjoy my visits to the Love Hong Kong teams during the next weeks, however. With other campaign co-ordinators I travelled all over the territories and islands and, usually, joined in whatever activities they happened to be involved in at the time. On the Fourth of July, Mee Un and I hopped a hydrofoil out to the two teams working on the Portuguese island of Macao.

Macao is a condensed version of Hong Kong Central, if poss-ible even more crowded and choked by traffic fumes. The key to its attraction is its casinos. Since all forms of gambling – except for horse-racing – are prohibited in Hong Kong, Macao can always count on drawing an enthusiastic clientele.

Our teams elected to spend the evening downtown, talking to people on the streets and outside the island's popular McDonald's restaurant. The cross-section of nationalities we encountered was quite remarkable, and many passers-by seemed happy enough to stop and chat. In the course of that night's conversations three men and women took their first step of faith in Jesus Christ. We thought it was time well spent.

A few days later Mee Un and I ferried out to another outlying island. Cheung Chau, in contrast to overcrowded Macao, bans the use of cars entirely. Its 50,000 residents get around by foot, bicycle and inexpensive sampan water taxis.

Our team in Cheung Chau had found folk religion deeply embedded among members of this fishing community. Shrines appear everywhere – at the foot of trees that spirits are believed to inhabit, on the streets and in homes.

Cheung Chau's annual Bun Festival is an event that draws visitors from far and wide. No one is quite sure if its purpose is to placate the spirits of ancestors murdered by pirates, or animals killed over the course of a year, but during the festival the eating of fish or meat is outlawed. Paper money, cars and houses are ceremonially burned and different foods

– including three high towers covered with sweet buns – are offered to appease the ghosts' hunger.

Unsurprisingly, the team was finding it hard going. Camped in the humble church that hosted them, they battled with mosquitos and even rats. Spiritual resistance was strong. None the less, they all agreed they had learned a lot. If nothing else, this international team knew they had injected some much-needed encouragement into the small body of believers on Cheung Chau.

By the end of the Love Hong Kong outreach, a total of three thousand individuals had prayed with team members or expressed a serious interest in learning more about Jesus Christ. Each of these contacts would be followed up by local churches.

Before leaving the country I asked for an interview with mission leader Stella Chan. Besides establishing O.M.'s work in the territory, Stella served with one of the oldest and largest churches in the territory. Only three years before, the 3,000-member Hong Kong Baptist Church had moved into new quarters. It was now housed in a soaring fifteen-floor sanctuary and office building which, according to Stella, was completed without the need for a loan. The project had even left a healthy bank balance!

Most impressive to me was the fact that the church was not an empty showplace but a caring community centre, reaching through its members to people across the world and in its own back yard. Stella's pastoral responsibilities extended to meetings for village women and a visiting programme for hospitals and old folks' homes. She also travelled to neighbouring countries to assist where she could.

The best example of local church outreach that I witnessed in Hong Kong was a meeting organised monthly by local believers in front of Tin Hau Temple in Hong Kong Central. The Temple's courtyard is a traditional gathering place for card-playing, fortune-telling and drinking. Lit largely by the flickering glow of kerosene lamps and obscured by smoke and shadow, the scene resembles a movie set of hell.

Try to imagine several hundred Christians in front of the temple gates, bathed in a blaze of floodlights. Their voices and musical instruments are lifted in concerted praise to the God above gods. Two huge banners stretching overhead declare in Cantonese characters: 'Jesus Loves Temple Street'.

The contrast of light and darkness was stunning. The almost tangible sense of God using the praise of his people to overcome the darkness was unlike anything I had ever witnessed. And that feeling remained as believers began moving into the shadowy perimeters to distribute literature or talk.

On my last morning in Hong Kong I took a bus to Operation Mobilisation's tiny office in Kowloon. Canton Road, Kowloon, also happens to be the site of a wonderful Chinese market that boasts every delicacy from pigs' ears to chicken feet.

The first time I visited this market I happened to be enjoying a bowl of bean curd in sauce when the vendor suddenly took to his heels. I found myself obliged to chase the cart down the street in order to return my bowl! My giggling companion explained that the owner was probably unlicensed – and he had just spotted an approaching policeman.

To the Chinese, freshness in food is everything. Live chickens are slaughtered for customers on the spot. In restaurants, the diner may choose the fish he will eat while it is still swimming in the tank. In the medical realm, natural cures are much preferred over modern pharmaceuticals. The local apothecary makes extensive use of ancient root and herb recipes – perhaps even throwing in an occasional deer antler!

Since I had a few hours free before my lunch appointment with O.M.'s South-east Asia leader Rodney Hui, I left my bags in the office and took a walk. Nearby Reclamation Street was aptly named for its array of used metal parts and tools stockpiled for resale. I kept walking until I came to the Bird Market.

Songbirds, I had learned, were the number one pet in Chinese households – an understandable choice considering the general lack of floor space. Still, the idea of 'walking' birds rather than dogs was something quite new to me. I never quite got used to the spectacle of devoted bird owners carrying their caged pets along with them on the streets.

Hong Lok Street in Kowloon is devoted exclusively to the purchase and care of feathered friends. Here one can find magnificently fashioned wood and bamboo cages in every shape and size. Besides regular birdfeed, one can also buy live grasshoppers for one's pet. I felt sorry for the insects who tried to cling to me as I walked past: no doubt they were hoping for rescue. Owners traditionally feed these wretched insects to their birds with chopsticks. The most pampered pets get to chase down the grasshoppers with honeyed liquids, which supposedly sweeten the quality of their singing.

From Hong Lok Street I still had enough time to track down the Jade Market, which was off Temple Street. One peek into this fascinating tented city and I was lost. Necklaces, earrings and figurines carved in cool green stone were enticingly displayed by merchants all too willing to bargain. I squandered the last of my Hong Kong dollars on a necklace for my sister and, on an impulse, bought an interestingly figured pendant for myself.

Back at the office my Asian friends inspected my purchases and rolled their eyes.

'Debbie, do you know what the design on your amulet signifies?'

I looked blank, and they burst into laughter. 'It's a spirit sign! Used in folk worship.'

As they described the stone's symbolism in more detail I sighed. After Dr Liu's lecture no one in his right mind would want to keep such a souvenir. I handed it back for them to dispose of and went off with Rodney and his assistant, Ruth Lim. They soon consoled me with a farewell *dim sum* lunch.

Between the tasty hot snacks offered in individually covered baskets, I plied Rodney with questions. Why had he moved his family here from Singapore? How did he forecast the colony's future? How was the countdown going to affect mission activity?

'Irene and I moved to Hong Kong last year because we

thought it was the most strategic place in all of Asia,' he answered thoughtfully. 'There's a sense here of meeting a deadline. We want to invest in ways to make our work long-term, even if it closes to the outside in 1997. That's why we're looking for property to buy. We don't anticipate leaving.'

Rodney's optimism encouraged me. It reminded me of what Stella Chan had told me in her interview.

'I don't think there will be a radical change in 1997, just a gradual one. And Jesus never changes! Whatever happens, the Lord calls us to be faithful . . . We are not to be afraid ahead of time.'

And that, I reflected, was a pretty good policy for any of us to follow in this uncertain world.

20

Delays and deliverances

He that will learn to pray, let him go to sea.
George Herbert
Jacula Prudentum, 1651

It was 8 December 1991: the scheduled day of departure for
the *Logos II* from Montevideo, Uruguay. I was in the ship's
laundry helping my German friend Bärbel sort the mountain
of dirty clothing brought back by the drydock outreach teams,
when First Engineer Elon Alva stuck his head in.

'Those cleaning supplies in the loft should be made more
secure,' he advised Bärbel. 'We've heard there's a Force Six
to Eight storm rising outside the harbour tonight.'

Shortly afterwards Captain Dyer's voice came over the PA
system. He had decided to postpone sailing until the next
morning because of the deteriorating weather and a port
strike.

I groaned. One more delay to cap a whole baffling series
of incidents and accidents that had dogged the *Logos II* in
Montevideo. The first crisis developed when the ship's nurse
was diagnosed with malaria – a leftover of her visit to Africa
a few months before. Uruguayan health officials, unused to
seeing malaria cases, panicked and closed the ship. Only
one or two hours elapsed before they remembered that
malaria was noncontagious and reopened the vessel, but
the damage was already done. Radio, TV and newspaper
publicity triggered an epidemic of cancellations by individuals

174

and groups, including 2,000 of the 6,000 school children expected.

During the next weeks two pregnant women on the staff suffered a miscarriage and near-miscarriage respectively, and a back problem sent an American man home for possible surgery. A mysterious bacterial infection hospitalised an engineer's wife and a traffic accident left the First Officer's wife, Klaudia de Jonge, with a broken collarbone and cracked pelvis.

Then the drydock yard postponed *Logos II*'s mandatory maintenance checkup, pushing the dates from 11 to 18 November and finally to 27 November, throwing the future port schedules into chaos. Dates carefully publicised in advance by posters, newspapers and flyers were suddenly invalid.

I had been invited to the *Logos II* that November to record her voyage around the southern cone of South America. It was an exciting assignment for any writer, but for me the voyage held particular significance. Our route was charted to take us from the Atlantic to the Pacific through the Beagle Channel – directly past the wreckage of my old ship, the first *Logos*. A special cameraman and O.M.'s International Co-ordinator, George Verwer, were also planning to be on board for this historic passage.

My arrival from London had been designed to dovetail with the *Logos II*'s departure from Uruguay. The delay in drydocking meant that, instead of going straight to the ship, I found myself deposited for ten days in a church camp outside Montevideo. I was less than enchanted at this turn of events. Uruguay is rich in natural beauty, but I did not count mosquitos, snakes and iguanas among its charms.

Then the big blow fell. Leaders decided that because of all the schedule delays, they should discard the plan to take the ship through the Beagle Channel and use the Strait of Magellan instead. This would save some sailing time and would allow the *Logos II* to keep most of her programme intact in Punta Arenas, Chile. But it meant, of course, that we would no longer be passing the shipwrecked *Logos*.

I was devastated. So was the cameraman who had already

flown in from Australia. The coming together of *Logos* and *Logos II* was to have been a poignant climax of the ship's time in South America. I could only hope there was another story waiting for me somewhere else along the way.

When the *Logos II* finally got under way from Montevideo on 9 December the staff and crew gave a concerted sigh of relief. New recruits looked happily forward to three days of sun and sea. The more seasoned sailors were more cautious. Ahead of us lay the 'Roaring Forties'. Crossing this latitude without running into at least one major storm would be too good to be true.

Sure enough, by our second night the ship was tossing so heavily it was almost impossible not to be thrown from our bunks. Sleep was out of the question. My closet door flew open and the contents of shelves were thrown to the floor. All over the ship ominous crashes and bangs indicated something of the chaos that would greet us in the morning.

By that time many of my shipmates were too far gone in seasickness to care. Those of us who were still able to stagger to breakfast compared notes and inspected the rest of the ship. The neatly laid out book holds were in the worst shape: a glance inside revealed that hundreds of books, posters and pens had been pitched helter-skelter into the aisles, the piles growing steadily higher as the violent motion continued.

As we met for prayer in the main lounge, tall stacks of chairs toppled over. Heavy plant pots slid from one end of the room to the other and some overturned. Pots, pans and food burst from pantry cupboards and refrigerators. A meat slicer took a dive down the galley steps.

Several times during that long day I stood on deck, fascinated by the fierceness and majesty of the waves around us. At the same time I could not help wondering, once or twice, if the ship might just keep on rolling so far over on to her side that she could not recover herself. A vessel in calm weather sits more or less at a right angle – 90° – to the water. It was just as well I didn't know our bridge instruments had registered a roll of 22°.

Radio officer Ian Currey reported that our destination of Puerto Madryn, Argentina, was also in trouble. A whole year's rainfall had deluged the town in only two days, leaving flooded streets and stranded cars. Ships in the harbour had gone aground. Did this mean the *Logos II* would have to cancel her plans for a stop in Puerto Madryn as well?

We anchored outside the harbour late on the night of 11 December. The next day the damage to the pier was assessed to see if it was safe to go in. Not until early evening did the wind drop sufficiently for us to proceed to our berth. It was then we received a jolt, for in the precise spot where our ship would have been tied up – had we not been delayed an extra night in Uruguay – was the clearly visible hull of another vessel, buried underwater.

Two ships had been sunk during the storm, three others had been cast ashore. Our times were in God's hand.

Following a successful week of conferences in Puerto Madryn the *Logos II* turned her back on the Atlantic Ocean and sailed through the Straits of Magellan. By mid-afternoon we were tying up in Punta Arenas, Chile, the southernmost city in the world. It gave me a strange feeling to be back. Exactly four years ago we had celebrated our last Christmas aboard the *Logos* in Punta Arenas. Two weeks later the *Logos* hit the rocks and we were airlifted back as refugees.

The arrival of the *Logos II* provided a good story for the Chilean media. More importantly, our visit was a song of triumph for God's church. Christians had been praying a long time for this replacement ship. Now the evidence of their faith was visible.

The need for prayer was not over yet. That first Sunday of our ten-day visit I was awakened early by the *Logos II*'s uneasy motion and the sound of something knocking hard against the hull. I dressed hurriedly and grabbed my camera. The gale we had been warned about the night before was fully upon us.

On deck I stepped into the full force of the storm and found myself in the company of Chilean sailors. What in the world were they doing on our ship? I wondered dazedly. Then I noticed the Navy patrol boat alongside which the sailors were attempting to secure. It was the sound of this boat banging into the *Logos II* that had jarred me from sleep.

All around us the sea and wind roared with incredible savagery. Huge, dirty waves were hurling themselves against the harbour's small fleet of fishing boats. Some of them – including a twin of the patrol boat snugging up to us – had already been cast on to the shore. The rain was driving into my face so I abandoned my picture-taking attempts and went inside.

Logos II staff huddled by the windows of the main lounge, stunned by the drama they had already witnessed and pointing to the wreckage on the beach. When I climbed the companionway to the bridge I could only look out in silent horror. All the cheerfully painted fishing craft that just yesterday had been tied to the pier in front of us – the same boats we had walked past, waving to men enjoying their lunches in the sunshine – had been smashed to splinters.

Immediately in front of us, in the berth originally intended for the *Logos II*, one of two large trawlers was aground. The other one was being saved from the same fate by the action of our crew, who were winching it free.

Suddenly I was afraid. Several of the largest ships tied near us, including a Navy warship, were quitting the pier to ride out the storm at anchor. Our own captain would have to decide whether to do the same. Winds were touching Force Nine strength and half a dozen of our heavy mooring lines had snapped since early morning. But how could we safely move away with a boat sunk immediately behind us, two trawlers ahead and a fishing boat anchored close to our port side? We were in no danger, everybody kept saying. But I remembered hearing those same words in another storm on another *Logos*. I decided to pack a small survival bag – just in case.

For hours we watched and prayed for the fate of the

small blue fishing boat nearest us, tugging like a frightened mare at her mooring. A man and his dog were aboard, fighting desperately to save it, but as, one by one, the other boats succumbed to the fury of the gale it seemed the little blue vessel was also doomed. She began to list heavily. The man attempted to start the engine, but a giant wave slammed over the deck. The engine stopped and I saw the fisherman emerge waving a red flag of distress. There was nothing we – or anyone else – could do. Before our horrified eyes the boat went over.

Oh God! Dear God, save him! I cried soundlessly, tears streaming down my face as I strained to catch sight of the small figure struggling in the waves. From the pier a Navy frogman jumped into the sea in a valiant rescue attempt. Both men were swept inexorably towards the concrete sea wall where it was almost certain they would be killed. But, somehow, they were not. At the very last moment rescuers stationed at the sea wall managed to drag the two men to safety. We all went limp with relief.

The *Logos II* remained at her berth and came through the storm without damage. We were singularly fortunate. Altogether that terrible Sunday thirteen boats around us were sunk and eight more went aground. A sailor in a Navy supply ship across the pier was seriously injured when a container shifted, crushing his arm. Three other men were drowned. One of them, an American officer named Mike, had visited our ship just the afternoon before.

That Christmas of 1991, celebrated a few days after the storm, held a heightened significance for most of us. Perhaps we were more keenly aware of how much we actually had when we had Jesus, and why it was so important, with life and death so close together, that the rest of the world should know him, too.

The *Logos II* was awarded $10,000 for salvage of the fishing trawlers. Our mission leaders agreed that the money should be turned over to local families who had suffered the greatest losses from the storm. It seemed like a small way to repay the hospitality the community had shown us, both now and in the past.

Before leaving port we arranged a Dinner of Thanks specifically to honour families who had hosted the shipwrecked crew members of the *Logos*. At an official reception, Captain Dyer presented the Chilean Naval Commodore of the Antarctic Fleet with a plaque of appreciation for the Navy's rescue efforts.

An American working in Punta Arenas told me he had spent three days aboard the wreck of the *Logos* in 1988, assisting the Chilean Navy's salvage operations. He had passed through the Beagle Channel several times since then and, in fact, was able to produce a photograph of the *Logos* taken only a few months before. Though most of her white paint was gone, she was still readily identifiable. It felt strange to look at that photo. It was like seeing the body of a familiar person after the spirit has departed from it. The Navy in Punta Arenas, we knew, was still using one of the *Logos* vans; and everything else redeemable had been stripped, including the parquet flooring and inlaid designs of the ship's stairwell and dining room.

Yet even after her death the old warrior had managed to pass on something of eternal value. We learned that when one of the Navy divers involved in the salvage operations returned home, he was given some of the undamaged books from the book exhibition as a gesture of thanks. The man gave them all away – except for one. Through reading that book he decided to put his trust in Christ and today he is a leading member of his church.

Liliana was another of the *Logos*'s hidden treasures. Four years before she had stolen two Bibles from the book exhibition, thinking they might be valuable enough to sell. As she opened one copy and began to read it, however, she was suddenly completely convinced of the reality of God. Eventually Liliana abandoned her involvement with prostitution, drugs and the occult. She began a new life in Christ. She told the pastor of her church that before being baptised she wanted to ask forgiveness for her theft from the crew of the *Logos II*. When Liliana shared her story with us the forgiveness she sought was freely given. Tears of celebration flowed. The evening seemed a fitting climax – and benediction – to our visit to the ends of the earth.

21

The long and short of it

You have to be thin to be a Chileno.
Otherwise you fall off!

Remark to John Gunther,
Inside South America

The opening of the New Year found the *Logos II* gliding past
the southernmost tip of the South American mainland. The
scenery was spectacular: deepwater fjords and mountains
with trailing cascades, glaciers, the waterspouts of passing
whales, vibrant-hued sunsets. The only troubled patch in four
days' sailing was the rough passage through the appropriately
named *Golfo de Penas* – Gulf of Misery!

Southern Chile has to be one of the prizewinning beauty
spots of the world. The skyline above the small town where we
tied up next was crowned by majestic volcanos, snow-covered
even in midsummer and shrouded in cloud on all but the
clearest days.

Puerto Montt is primarily a fishing community, unused to
accommodating vessels as large as the *Logos II*. We were
afraid we might run into trouble keeping a berth and we
did. When my church team returned to the quayside that
first Sunday we discovered the ship had sailed without us!
Fortunately she hadn't gone far and a boat was despatched
to pick us up. The *Logos II* had to lie at anchor for most of the
remainder of the visit. A small fleet of local boats was hastily
hired to ferry the public to and fro. In spite of the fact that all

but one of the conferences had to be cancelled, we welcomed a ten-day total of about eighteen thousand visitors.

On-shore evangelism presented a further challenge. Picture the expedition one evening that required two launches with eighteen of us wedged between guitars, countless boxes of used clothing, a film projector and generator, plus tracts. After a rendezvous with local church people in the poorest section of town, we set up a one-of-its-kind hair cutting salon. Nine qualified barbers wielded their scissors on happy residents while the rest of us sang or visited each house to invite everyone to an evangelistic film show. It wasn't long before we had all the men, women, children and dogs we could handle.

Andreas, who was a professional hair stylist back in Switzerland, admitted to me later that he hadn't been looking forward to this adventure. 'I didn't want to cut hair in that place, I knew we would find dirt and lice. But I began to work, and suddenly—' a smile of wonder lit his face '—the joy came! It was a practical way to show the love of Jesus.'

The next day, ship leaders gave permission for me to accompany five ship engineers to the isolated island of Chiloe. The only expatriate missionary on the island had requested a team to travel around showing the *Jesus* film, possibly to other islands as well. Since the missionary was a lady, I took a chance that she wouldn't mind the addition of a female reporter on the team.

Ellie Lowell turned out not only to be an American but a fellow 'Mainiac'. She declared she was 'tickled pink' to have a woman along from her own home state.

Over the years I have glimpsed a whole range of lifestyles and spent nights in drastically different types of accommodation, but Ellie's simple way of life moved me profoundly. Her spartan rented room, shared with her Chilean helper Miriam, served for all their living and sleeping purposes. The women had no refrigerator and a two-ring gas burner provided the only means of cooking. Water for drinking and dishwashing had to be fetched from the owner's kitchen facilities – then disposed of through a window. They were also given access to the owner's cold water bath and toilet.

Ellie gave me her own single bed despite my protests and doubled up with Miriam. January was summertime below the equator, but in that latitude of Chile it was always chilly. The small room's wooden floor and walls were not solid proof against the draught.

'How do you heat this place in the winter?' I asked one morning, huddled under wool blankets while Ellie boiled tea. 'I bet it's freezing!'

'Oh, we leave the burner on sometimes.' She smiled cheerfully. 'The flame helps a little.'

The woman's zeal amazed me. Not content with running Chiloe's only Christian bookshop, Ellie spent much of her time on the road, taking books and tapes to more remote areas by bus or boat. Although she works without the support of any mission agency and earns the slenderest of incomes, she hopes at least to provide a Bible to every island home.

The impact of the films we showed during our four days together convinced Ellie that she needed to add a video ministry to her other projects. Financial support did not seem to worry her. 'If God wants it, he'll help to make it happen as he has made everything else happen!' was her confident attitude.

When the team drove back to the ship, Ellie and Miriam decided to come with us and spend a night on board before going to Santiago for supplies. *Logos II* leaders asked her to share her vision for Chile with the rest of the crew that evening. By the time we met again her face was glowing like a child's at Christmas.

'I'm marking this day on my calendar!' she laughed. 'I've had a hot shower for the first time in a year! And cereal for breakfast! It's so great to speak English again and share with you all. God has really used you to be an encouragement to me.'

Pioneering spirits like Ellie's were the living evidence of something author Hal Borland once wrote: 'A frontier is never a place; it is a time and a way of life. Frontiers pass, but they endure in their people.' I was very glad that we had met.

On a sunny mid-January afternoon the deck crew cast off the *Logos II*'s mooring ropes once again. Two tugboats nosed our ship past the towering cross on the hill overlooking Puerto Montt, and another port of call was history.

Temperatures climbed as we headed north up Chile's long, 2,650-mile coastline. Approaching Talcahuano, the country's naval headquarters, we wrinkled our noses at the increasingly obnoxious breeze blowing our way.

'What on earth is it?' we demanded as the ship continued ploughing her way through hundreds of floating seagulls and pelicans. To our dismay we learned that we were about to spend the next three weeks in the country's most polluted harbour. Talcahuano was a regrettable example of what happens when factory discharges go uncontrolled. We were convinced that if any of us fell overboard we would disintegrate within minutes. At night, when the ship's air-conditioning was switched off and outside air circulated, it was like waking up in a cesspool.

Fortunately the enormous welcome by the local residents did much to compensate for the unfriendly nose-zone layer. Some seventy-eight thousand came aboard to buy books and to sit in conferences that included 'Woman to Woman', 'Kingdom of the Cults', and 'The Christian Marriage'. On Friday nights the aft lounge was transformed into an English café with tables and chairs, coffee, soft music and relaxed conversation. Local people were invited to practise their English with crew members – like me – not fluent in Spanish. I thought it was a great idea.

The first night I sat by a young guy named Carlos who said he had been a Christian for only a few months. For eight years prior to that he'd played for a Satanic band. Carlos explained that his group was part of a large network of Satan worshippers that stretched throughout southern Chile. Contact with a Christian girl and her church had helped him break free. Now the young musician was rebuilding ties with his family and, as he put it, composing music for Jesus.

Myrna and Lorena were my second 'customers', but their

grasp of English was even worse than my Spanish. Conversation was tough. Then a short music video called 'Secret Ambition' came on the mounted screens, catching the girls' attention. They listened intently afterwards as I tried to explain more of the message behind the video. When I finally asked if they were interested in inviting Jesus Christ into their lives, they promptly said 'Yes'! I was certain they hadn't understood my stumbling Spanish and excused myself, intending to find a translator.

'But we understood!' they protested, smiling. 'We understand everything!' And it actually appeared they did. They returned to talk with me several times after that evening, and before the ship left Talcahuano the girls presented me with a copper plaque of the Last Supper. They had engraved on it, 'To Debbie from Lorena and Myrna – Thanks for to be our friend'.

The homeless bands of children roaming the streets of South America have recently become the focus of international concern. I hadn't been with the ship in Brazil, but I knew the crew had been deeply affected by their contacts with children in that country. In Chile, however, we saw little evidence of street kids. I wondered why until a group of us went to hold a programme in a large men's prison near Concepción. In the juvenile section we found ourselves looking into the faces of little boys of only eight and nine years old.

We asked the warden what their crimes were. He shrugged. Some had committed no crime. They were orphans. Were the homeless children imprisoned together with those who had broken the law? Yes, he replied, they were one big family. He seemed rather proud of the fact, showing us around neat but stark dormitories, an adequate kitchen. There was even a classroom although, he apologised, it was guards – not qualified teachers – who ran it. I saw no women anywhere.

A boy loitering nearby, in his mid-teens, looked at me with mute appeal. I asked how long he had been inside. Six years, he said. He would not be released until he was eighteen. I wanted to cry and put my arms around him, around them all. What chance did they have? Who could begin to heal their terrible hurts?

On our final day in port a local missionary rounded up a dozen children still living in the rough. When they came aboard the *Logos II* they were awestruck. Eagerly they swallowed the sandwiches and cookies brought from the galley, tried on the used clothing we had collected. Then they settled down for a film. The movie was about two teenage gang members, one of whom meets the Lord and ends up taking the jail rap for his friend. The kids were rivetted. Love was an alien concept in their world, especially the love of God. But perhaps for the first time some of these throwaways of society began to understand that in his sight, at least, they were of infinite value.

Pollution of God's perfect creation was everywhere, I decided – it just took different forms in different places. But God had invested an awful lot in this planet of his. As long as he hadn't written it off, I didn't see how we could, either.

22

Home is the sailor

To reach the port of heaven we must sail, sometimes with the wind and sometimes against it. But we must sail, not drift or lie at anchor.

Oliver Wendell Holmes

My final voyage aboard the *Logos II* took us from Talcahuano to Valparaiso in less than twenty-four hours. The world famous harbour was even more beautiful than I remembered: a wide half-circle overlooked by steep surrounding hills. The continuous traffic of cargo ships moving in and out of the port made our own vessel look rather insignificant. We were reassured, however, by the raft of TV crews and other media personnel awaiting our arrival. I plunged into my duties as press officer for the last time.

Following Sunday morning's church service I toyed with several possibilities for employing my final afternoon. The nearby tourist town of Vina del Mar was tempting – an ideal place to catch a few rays of South American sunshine before facing the bleak mid-winter of London. Or perhaps I should look for souvenirs to take home. A voice over the speaker system suddenly interrupted.

'PEOPLE ARE NEEDED TO PARTICIPATE IN AN OPEN AIR THIS AFTERNOON. IF YOU ARE AVAILABLE PLEASE REPORT TO THE AFT LOUNGE!'

Flesh and spirit wrestled for control. *What's the matter*

with you, are you here to do a job or not? A chance to do something significant with your last day and you want to go to the BEACH?

I crept into the back of the aft lounge. Probably a hundred people would show up and they wouldn't need me anyway.

'Debbie!' The evangelism leader pounced as I entered, seizing my arm. I smiled weakly. 'How about doing a sketchboard?'

Within half an hour we were hoofing our way to the nearby craft market. The programme attracted such a huge audience that we decided to repeat it – right in front of the ship where some of that afternoon's 12,700 visitors were lining up.

I had barely enough time to wash the paint off my hands and grab a bite of supper before rushing off again with my evening church team. On the platform the local translator leaned over to whisper, 'Do you know those young people sitting near the front?' I started to shake my head and then realised who they were: the new *Logos II* recruits, just arrived from Europe! They were staying on shore while they received orientation and training and hadn't yet been introduced to the rest of the crew.

How strange, I thought. Here it is their first Sunday in Chile and it's my last. We'll never even get to know each other! Suddenly I was overwhelmed with the desire to tell them something of all they had to look forward to.

It seemed more like a lifetime than ten weeks since I had hauled my own baggage up the gangway in Montevideo. My mind and heart were still reeling from 3,200 sea miles – down the 'Roaring Forties' of the Atlantic, through the Strait of Magellan to the Pacific and halfway up the other side of the continent. I wanted to share with these new recruits what it felt like to burn under the tropical sun and then shiver in the hostile winds of the Chilean Antarctic; to gaze at the splendour of snow-frosted volcanos, of glaciers and waterfalls that ran like silver ribbons down the forested back of the Andes; to trace the Southern Cross, flung like jewels against the midnight sky; to sail to the very end of the earth.

If only I could communicate to these newcomers what an

extraordinary privilege it was to laugh and weep and pray and work with strangers until they were forged into forever friends; to touch the wounds of a bleeding world, and watch God reach through us – imperfect, ordinary as we are – to heal some of its wounds and build his kingdom.

I wished that I could urge all these young men and women in front of me to seize every opportunity, no matter how uncertain they were of their abilities, to preach God's Good News in town squares and share their hope with people in prisons and hospital wards and churches and conferences. I wanted for them the satisfaction of rattling over dusty miles to show the *Jesus* film to isolated islanders. I wanted them to make a fool of themselves in Spanish – as I had – and see that the Holy Spirit can work in spite of it.

I wanted to reassure these raw recruits that the ship really is worth the money they've had to raise, the homesickness and seasickness they will endure. The heat and cold and cramped quarters and – yes – sheer weariness; because, as they will soon discover, there is little 'romance of the seas' when you're keeping watch in the grease and noise of an engine room, or scrubbing public toilets, or folding the endless laundry of two hundred men, women and children.

I wanted to show them the evidence. Let them talk to Maria, the prostitute who hung around after an open air to ask if salvation was really for her; or put their arms around Juan, the drug-addicted street kid who couldn't stop weeping when he realised that Someone loved him enough to die for him; I wanted them to look into the eyes of Erna, the despairing, near-suicidal mother and wife who picked up a discarded ship tract and discovered a reason to live.

Then I smiled, because I knew I didn't have to tell these new *Logos II* arrivals any of these things. For they would discover their own special miracles. They would meet their own Marias and Juans and Ernas and hundreds more like them in the next two years of their lives.

For them, the voyage had just begun.